Shannon Olson

It's Called a Trout Stamp Not a Food Stamp

Acknowledgment

First of all I would like to thank God for blessing me with such a great life. I have been very fortunate to be able to spend countless hours outdoors chasing my dreams. I would also like to thank my family and friends for supporting me in whatever crazy ideas I have at the time and helping me through the bad. And then there is Jenny, if not for her I would have never attempted this book. Her motivation and assistance was a Godsend and will never be forgotten. And finally, Thank You, if you are reading this right now your helping me live my dream. I hope you enjoy reading it as much as I have enjoyed living and writing it.

Table of Contents

Bungee Fishing 1

Horny Toad 11

It's Called Hunting, Not Killing...................19

Lost...31

Old Bird Dog...41

Quack Addict...53

Sand Bass...71

It's Called a Trout Stamp Not a Food Stamp....79

Four Wheels and No Brains...........................95

You're Not From Around Here Are Ya..........103

Sentimental Nature...................................117

Hog Wild...125

The River is Rising 135

Port Isabel...143

Round One...157

Prologue

The great outdoors is a place where almost anything can happen. A great place to spend time with people we love and at the same time a great place to get away when you need time to yourself. This book is a few stories of some great times I have survived. They are from times more current and from times past. Some are funny and some are sad, but all of them are real. I tried to express myself how I really talk, think and act, so my grammar and political correctness may not always be what it should be. However, it's how I am and I wanted to be as close to who I am in my writings. So enjoy yourself as you read about all the outings and memories of a young country kid who even after growing up has tried to stay a kid at heart.

Bungee Fishing

Duct tape, bailing wire, bungee cords and zip ties are all things I am very familiar with. After all I am a country boy from Southwest Oklahoma, and if something is broke you should be able to easily fix it with one of those four things. So when a buddy of mine asked me to go bungee fishing I was somewhat concerned. Bungee fishing? This was beginning to sound along the lines of snipe hunting. So of course I said, "hell Yeah I want to go."

Now we were going to fish for these so called monster catfish in the Red River of Oklahoma. So all I could do was laugh. As a child I fished the river and caught a lot of catfish in the two-pound range but no so called 'monsters' were ever caught by me in the river. And using bungee cords? I was really thinking my chain was being pulled.

But I did as my buddy asked me to and purchased bungee cords, caution tape, tent stakes and three hundred pound test fishing line and the biggest hooks that I could find. As I am getting the gear gathered up I am only wondering what kind of sick joke is about to be played on me. But I have a sense of humor as good as the next guy. So I am thinking this should be interesting, but in the back of my mind I'm thinking how paybacks are hell.

So I meet up with my buddy at his house

and we head to the river. I have my gear and he
has gathered up the bait. So the two of us and
his daughter head to the Red River that borders
Oklahoma and Texas just south of the town of
Davidson, Oklahoma. We go through this very
sandy brushy trail that appears to have been an
ATV trail winding through the trees to the
northern bank of the Red River. When we get
there the river is not at all what I was expecting
to see for these alleged monster catfish to be
living in. So I am really thinking that the joke is
about to begin. We start unloading our
Bronco's. Both of us had Ford Bronco II's for our
fishing wagons, or as his daughter called them
our 'jungle trucks.' We get the gear out and get
set up. We get a campfire lit, some chairs set up
and some lighting ready as darkness is
approaching.

My buddy's daughter had come with us
and she couldn't have been four at the time. We
did the most important part of that trip and got
her all geared up. She had snacks and
marshmallows on sticks to roast over the fire. I
am really not sure what is about to happen but
my buddy is positive that we will catch as he
called them 'huge fish.' However, from where I
am standing I can't picture that the water in the
river where we are at is over two or three feet
deep.

I have seen pictures of these huge catfish
that people have caught hand fishing or

noodling, but I am thinking that they were in huge holes in deep water. Not in the shallow river water like this. I am starting to realize that my friend is sincere and he has his mind set on this place and that this is the place to fish. I am all for it. My buddy is not much of a bull shitter and has always been a straight shooter with me. So he must know something about these big fish that I surely have yet to figure out.

We take our gear that he instructed me to get and we rig these 'limb lines' out of a bungee cord. It consists of a three foot rubber bungee cord with the metal hooks clamped shut making a figure eight at each end of the bungee cord. Then attach about a ten-foot piece of three hundred pound test fishing string to the bungee cord hook that has been clamped shut. There is a one-ounce slip sinker on the line and then the biggest fishing hook I have ever used is tied on. These hooks were as thick as three metal coat hangers and every bit of four inches long. So we make several of these contraptions and I am starting to see the genius of his idea. I have seen people use salt cedar sticks for limb lines and they are always tangled and take a bunch of room and are only good for one season. These gadgets only took a little space and were reusable season after season.

So after we rig up several he gets the cooler of bait out. In the cooler are some perch that were the size of my hand. When I say hand

I mean my fingers and all. And there were also
some two-pound carp. Now I have fished most
all of my life but most of what I have ever caught
was about the size of the bait we were using. So
I have to admit at this point I am beginning to
become pretty damn excited.

We start to place our bungee lines up and
down the river, staking each with a ten inch tent
stake with a piece of caution tape attached to the
stake so we could easily locate them when
checking in the dark. As we are setting them I
am figuring we will cut the bait into chunks but,
nope! We use the two-pound carp whole with
the hook through the back of the fish for bait.
We get all the lines we made set out, which is
probably two dozen or so, on the northern bank
over an area not much more than two hundred
yards. We then go back to the camp fire and rig
up a couple of poles and cast them out. Then we
sit and roast marshmallows and hot dogs over
the fire with his daughter. From where I am at,
life couldn't get much better.

We sat and shot the bull and told stories
to his daughter. We talked to each other about
how screwed up the world was and our plans to
fix it. This part of the story kind of sucks. My
buddy and I were extremely close friends both
serving our communities as law enforcement
officers, but because of small town politics we no
longer speak. Anyway we sit for probably thirty
minutes and I am asking him when do we check

the lines? He said to be patient that we will know when we get a bite, and that if an hour or so goes by we will check the bait.

The first hour goes by and nothing. I don't really care. I am enjoying the break from work and the company, plus the roasted marshmallows are not too bad either.

We go check the bait and it's all still alive and we haven't lost any as of yet. So we go back to the fire. As were sitting there you can hear the coyotes howling at the moon in all directions around us. The moon is full and there is enough of a breeze that the mosquitoes are not trying to carry us away. You can hear splashing in the water and some other strange noise of some sort that to this day after years of fishing on the river I have never figured out. I am guessing it was a beaver or some other water mammal, hell for all I know it could have been big foot.

So we continue to shoot the bull and all of a sudden a huge splash happens about fifty yards from us. I am ridiculously excited and race down to see what it is. We race down to the line and there is about a ten-pound channel catfish on the bungee line. Now that is a good size fish but my buddy is disappointed and it's not what I would call a monster either. I was proud to successfully catch it on a bungee cord, but still couldn't believe that even a ten-pound fish was in this shallow water.

At this point I am starting to believe that

my fishing buddy knows what he is doing and I am super excited and every splash I see or hear I want to run down the bank of the river to see what it is. For the next few hours about every ten to twenty minutes there is a large splash and we would go check it and it would be either a channel catfish or a flat head catfish on the line. Every one of the catfish would be in the five to ten pound range. I am happy with that but again; I still don't think their monsters by any count.

My fishing buddy is starting to get defensive and continues to explain to me that if you use big bait you never get quite as many bites but you only catch big fish. So he continues to tell to me to be patient. He preaches to me trying to convince me that there are in fact 'monsters' in this water. I am starting to give him shit and tell him that the water is not even deep enough, for the fish he keeps talking about, to be able to even swim through.

About this time I hear a splash. Not like before, this time it was really loud and continuous, and it sounded very close to where we were. I get up and go look and I am in total shock. I mean for real, I am in shock, not just surprised or anything I am in SHOCK! I am not sure what it is but it's less than twenty feet from me and it very well could be the Loch Ness Monster. I know this is a story but I am not exaggerating this thing at all, it was huge. I start to walk towards it and in the back of my mind I am thinking what the hell I am going to do with it when I get there. I am trying to act tough like this is normal fishing and not be too excited but I am scared to death to pick up a fish that could eat my extremities.   After all I am not very much bigger than this fish.   But as fate would have it as I approach this thing jumps one more time and swims away. I am not sure if it was God teasing me, or saving me from embarrassing myself, but either way it did get away. I walk to the bungee line, still confused as to what just took place. As I look in amazement that the little tent stake held the bungee cord, I am in more amazement that the fish straightened the massive hook out. I was in a state of confusion. Hell that thing was huge. And to be able to straighten metal like it did, it had to be tough as hell. I wasn't real sure I wanted to be handling this thing or if I was even capable of doing so. The fact that the water this catfish was splashing around in was super shallow and its tail was hitting the sandbar out in the river was amazing. I paced the distance from the bank to the sandbar and it was four and a half feet and the water was only two feet deep, if that. I couldn't help but thinking over and over and over about what strength a fish had to have to straighten out a hook like it did. I was at a loss. I could be bait and was having a hard time convincing myself to get back into that water after seeing that. I do now believe my fishing partner. There are in fact monsters in the Red River.

I set a new hook and put the bent one in my pocket because no one would believe me how big that fish was other than by fishing buddy who was there with me. But think about it. Who is going to believe two guys who were together on a fishing trip and didn't bring any home? It would just be another 'the one that got away' story. I still have that hook.

So we get back to fishing and a short while later we hear another splash. We run down to the river and there is damn sure something big on the line again. It's about half as big as the last one but still a monster to me. I am running over towards it and I get up to it and it rolls over several times. To be honest I have not a clue what I am supposed to do. This fish is not even close to as big as the last one but I still have no clue how to pick the thing up or if I am even strong enough to. I am thinking to myself, where the hell do I even grab it?

So as my buddy is laughing at my chicken shit self he comes over and helps me grab the fish. Ok he doesn't help me; he grabs the fish. So he has this fish and he picks it up with his hand in its mouth and the fish is every bit as big as his daughter. We even took a picture of the fish being held up next to her and its tail was curled on the ground and its head was slightly above hers. I do not want any part of holding that thing, and his daughter is up there petting on it and grabbing it and sticking her hands in its mouth helping her dad carry it. She is really showing me how big a pansy I am being. Anyway we weigh the fish and it was forty three pounds. To this day it is the largest fresh water fish I have ever been able to catch. We caught several other fish that night with a total stringer weight of over one hundred and twenty pounds. And for that total weight, there were less than ten fish to hit that mark. I was astonished that creatures that big swim in such shallow water and what was even more shocking to me is that fish that big are in waters so close to home.

I am not much of a bait fisherman. I tend to only fish with a fly rod, but I do enjoy nights out on the river. This is the only fish I do fish for with bait. The greatest part of it is that the bait to catch the river fish is some of my favorite to catch with a fly rod.

One thing I have learned is no matter how big you think your britches are and no matter where your life leads you, nights at the river are good for your soul. I do a lot of fishing anywhere I can, and yes most of it is with a fly rod. However, being a simple country boy on the river with good friends and bungee cords is probably as good as most any fancy fly fishing trip I could ever take. More time on the river and less time talking politics would probably do a lot of people some good.

Horny Toad

I would have to say that what makes the outdoors most enjoyable for me is how the solitude and the one on one encounters with nature can trigger memories. It amazes me that the world has changed so much but out in 'Gods' country, it in a strange way stays the same.

It's the first of September so the sacred migration has begun here in Oklahoma. Me and a couple friends have got all of our crap loaded and are going to partake in the very first hunt of the season. After several days of being teased by large flocks of dove flying from highline wires to the mesquite bushes it is finally our moment to shine. It is this very same day year to year that egos are boosted with great shots or more likely than not new excuses are created about things being everything but our own faults when we miss what should be a super easy shot as the dove fly over us. 'Super Easy Shot,' anyone who has ever dove hunted knows that is not going to happen. Anyway the hunting was good and yes bad shots were took and even a large hairy tarantula decided up my leg was a good place to go for an afternoon stroll.

But all these things aside one event stood out to me. As we were unloading our gear to get set up on the small pond a very little horny toad

ran under the truck. I was doing everything in
my power to catch it just for a picture, as I hadn't
seen one in several years.

Growing up in Southwest Oklahoma,
seeing a horny toad was nothing special they
were everywhere but each year it seems that the
numbers of them are getting smaller and
smaller. All of the chemicals being sprayed on
the crops have damn sure taken its toll on the
horny toad. Now I say that, I have no data to
back up my assumption but to me it seems like
common sense that this is what has happened
with them. But either way seeing one now is
sure enough a rare enjoyable treat for me.

I may be getting older by my behaviors in
the woods. Meaning that I am way more
interested in seeing odd critters than shooting
mass numbers of birds. I have turned into a
trophy hunter. I am not out for the biggest or
the best animal in the woods. I just want to
share stories of encounters with others and have
mounts of animals that some people do not even
know exist. That's why this horny toad was so
damn neat for me.

I have lived in Oklahoma for almost two
and a half decades but as a young child I was
raised in Golden, Colorado and I never in those
young years ever noticed such a creature as a
horny toad. So when my mom got remarried
and we moved to Oklahoma I had the great
opportunity to observe my very first horny toad.

This day begins early in the morning in Sayre, Oklahoma in the back yard of our new home in a way different place than where I came from. Our new home had an old pen in the back yard that at some point may have held some kind of animal but as rusty and knocked down as the wire was this thing could not hold much of anything anymore. I am almost eight years old and damn sure didn't feel like moving boxes of stuff around and helping like I should have. To me playing in the boxes and getting in everyone else's way was way more fun and rewarding. But on this particular day I was taught a very long lasting lesson on karma. As all of my family is working on getting us moved in and settled into our new home I am the one carrying the boxes in the back and throwing them into the old rusted wire pen in the back yard until we are finished.

I start to carry all of the boxes out and piling them up inside the pen so that the wind won't blow them away. That was probably one of my first lessons of being an "okie". The wind does blow and blow and blow in Oklahoma and if you do not take precautions to keep things from blowing around you will soon spend all afternoon picking up loose items down the road from where you left them.

As with most everything else I did and still do I became very bored very fast with moving boxes. I soon started taking the boxes

and connecting them together and created this
elongated tunnel made from one box connected
to another to another. Wasting our supply of
shipping tape hooking them together so they
would stay attached when I was crawling
around inside of them. I began to get involved
with this so much that I had forgot that I was
supposed to be helping everyone else with the
moving. I had a pretty great imagination at that
age so hard telling what I thought I had made
out of all of the cardboard boxes. I can only
begin to think. Had I built a factory? A hospital?
A house? A fort? I can honestly say I don't
remember, but for the sake of the story I am
going to say a castle. As my young and
adventurous self am making my way through
the series of boxes until I get to the very last one,
probably at least ten, and in the back of my
castle looking me square in the eyes is a dragon.

Now I know I have a good imagination
but this is way too real to be all in my head. I'm
scared and I don't know what to do. This
dragon, dinosaur, hell I don't even know what I
think it is at this point but it is walking towards
me and I have nowhere to go. I am wishing
really bad at this point that I didn't use so much
of the packing tape securing this damn thing, so
good that I can't break out of it. I am not sure
what to do, but I at this point am willing to do
almost anything to get out of this card board
castle. And if it's not bad enough, this damn

dragon, dinosaur spiny creature begins to start spitting fire at me. I am so scared I am about to piss all over myself, but I somehow get the courage to run past this four and a half inch long monster that is reeking havoc on my castle, and has me trapped in the card board prison that just moments before was the finest card board castle in Oklahoma. I am crawling on all fours as if I am a new born baby as fast as any Olympic runner could move to get out of these boxes that are laid on their side and stand way too short for me to be able to stand up and just run out. So I finally get out of the boxes and all I see is fence. Now the fence is as tall as I am and not attached too much of anything to hold itself up. But for the safety of me and the world I make my escape and climb the fence and run into the house where everyone else is working.

So I go running to my mom and step dad screaming at the top of my lungs. "DINOSAUR, THERE IS A DINOSAUR OUTSIDE!!!!!!!!!!!!!!" Later in my life they said I had turned as white as a ghost when I ran into the house. But at this point in time they are looking at me like I had lost my ever loving mind. Looking back they probably were thinking I was huffing paint in them boxes. But I am so panicked and unable to explain this fire breathing creature that really is in the back yard and that I had just had a standoff with it, that they are beginning to believe that I had in fact seen something out there.   So both of my parents come outside to look and the gate to the pen is closed and is wired shut so neither of them believes me and are looking at me like I am full of crap again. So I begin in detail to explain how there is a dragon in the boxes, that the dragon had me trapped inside the boxes and when I tried to pass it to escape that it spit fire towards me but that I was brave and made my way past it and was able to jump over the fence. So my dad gives into my story and goes to look so that I will calm down. The boxes are all still attached so he has to go in them as well and he gets on all fours and crawls inside the cardboard tunnel bravely and sure enough he finds the dragon and begins to chase me out of the boxes laughing at me. So being the tough guy that I am I go running to mommy screaming for help. My dad approaches us and my mom doesn't even know what to think about this creature. I am somewhat relieved to prove to my parents that I wasn't full of crap but proving that would in fact prove that a dragon really did exist and that it lived in my own back yard.

Finally I start to calm down and my dad explains to me that what I thought was a dragon was in fact the first Texas Horned Lizard or also known as a "horny toad" that I had ever seen. He further told me that they spit blood not fire. I thought he was screwing with me about that as well but later in life I did some research and its true they do spit blood from their mouths as well is the sides of their eyes as a natural defense against canines. The "Blood" secretes some offensive taste that encourages canines to spit out a horned lizard if it ever gets it in its mouth.

So anyway, sitting back at the pond supposed to be dove hunting my mind has been wondering about to my dragon fight or stand off as a young child. The hunt ended up being a fairly good one but I wonder what my friends were thinking as I was sitting there day dreaming of fighting dragons. I hope that some of the thoughts I was having were not spoken out loud. If so my buddies may never want to go hunting with their "dragon slayer" buddy again.

It's Called Hunting, Not Killing

I am actually sitting in a deer stand on top of a canyon as I am writing this. To my North are a series of small canyons with spotted areas of mesquite and sagebrush and between that all you can see is staggering areas of Oklahoma red dirt. To my East is a pond, not a very large one but very alive and active. The pond is covered in duck week, surrounded by cattails and all around the cattails are various songbirds. The songbirds are flying in and out of the cattails with the grace of a dancer. To the South there is an area of prairie grass and a winter wheat field.

You can hear the songbirds whistling and the quail calling back their covey. In the small grassy area there is a doe and her two young fawns about two hundred yards from my stand on top of the canyon. The weather is pleasantly chilly but not cold. It is in my opinion the most perfect weather. I could sit here all day in this stand and look over the countryside and not even bring a gun. Just sit back and watch the amazing world we as humans are a very small part of.

I sit here hoping the buck of a lifetime will come within my guns range and my ability to shoot. Knowing that the possibility of that not happening is greater than it all coming together,

but regardless the outcome it doesn't matter.
Hunting is a relaxing, rewarding and refreshing
hobby to me, with or without a kill.

As I say this I observe two hunters sitting
on the fence line on the Eastern property line. I
am not sure where they are so I do not have a
safe backstop at a distance to my East. I came to
shoot for meat, so I don't care if I end up with a
doe or buck or both. However, if I want to take
a shot, I won't have a safe backstop because I
don't know exactly where the other hunters are.
The doe I saw earlier is getting spooked by the
presence of the other hunters and have ran off
into a group of trees by the prairie grass. My
buddy is in a tower stand about three hundred
yards to the Southeast of me. He texts me and
tells me to look to his East.

To his East I look with my binoculars and
I can see a very large bobcat crawling by the
fence line. The bobcat is about five hundred
yards away. Close enough to try to shoot but it is
still not furbearer season yet so it is only a brief
tease to my mind.

I then see the two hunters walking
towards their trucks. It is an hour and a half
away from legal shooting hours so I am not sure
what they are thinking. As they start walking
out I see a nice rack poke up on the top of the
pond dam East of me. I get my binoculars and
look and see a nearly perfect ten-point white tail
buck. He has good antler mass and a big body,

swollen up from the rut. He is no record but very worthy of being eaten.

I get my rifle out but the other hunters have not left yet and I don't want to shoot in their direction. So I wait, my heart is racing and I am starting to get the shakes. I happen to get this way almost every time I go deer or turkey hunting right before the shot. It's like the first time every time for me. I'm keeping an eye on the buck but I lose him. The other hunters are in their trucks driving off and I cannot see this buck anymore. My heart is still racing but starting to settle down. A couple minutes go by and he pops his head up again. This time he has walked right behind where our pickup was parked. When we parked we parked where we thought was out of the way. Which is about three hundred yards from the stands and this damn deer is right there and he will not move. And yes in the back of my mind I am thinking, "Just how much is a tailgate for a 2010 ford?"

I get my rifle out knowing I am fully capable of taking this shot if he will move away from the back of the truck where I know I can take a safe shot. The buck then moves forward, I am looking at him threw my scope, I push the safety to fire and get my sight picture on him and out of nowhere this damn buck decides to jump up and start chasing the doe from earlier. So this decent buck is there one minute and gone the next. I never see him again but the shakes, heart racing and pure thrill of it all was just as good and I know that there will always be another day.

Hunting is not like normal typical sports. There are no winners or losers. Killing an animal isn't always a victory and not killing one doesn't always mean failure.

My grandfather on my dad's side was a world class hunter and a professional taxidermist by trade. They lived in North Dakota right on the Canadian border in a neat old rock house on a lake that shared the Canadian border. In that house my grandfather had a museum with almost every kind of animal native to North America. It was kind of like a dead version of a North American Noah's ark.

My dad grew up hunting and was, from what I hear, quite a successful hunter at that. I still have his rifle that has killed seven deer. I have the original box of bullets that came with it and there are only seven missing from the box. So in my opinion, dad was a good hunter. I have a picture of dad with his last deer. A nice buck hanging in a tree with dad in front of it, dressed in his typical 1970's fashion holding a can of beer. I would always ask my dad to go hunting or to just take me fishing and he never would. Never, not one time did me and my real father ever go hunting or fishing together. It never made sense to me. A father and son bonding outdoors has been a tradition in our family and dad did not want any part of it. I didn't understand how something so rewarding and fun could just not interest him anymore.

As I got older dad came down with cancer and the last year of his life he underwent numerous surgeries to try to fight the cancer. I would sit for hours and hours in the hospital room or talk on the phone with him for hours and hours. We would talk about most everything you could imagine trying to make up for all the times we didn't have when I was younger, and one day we brought up hunting.

A conversation about hunting with dad was kind of taboo to me. He was so against it, so I figured that something between him and grandpa must have happened a long time ago and I didn't want to take a chance of rekindling the problem. But in the last months of dad's life he explained it so clearly to me that it all made perfect since.   That last deer that dad shot, the one I have a picture of him with, looked dad strait in the eyes and dad said it had tears in its eyes as dad pulled the trigger. As if it knew what was about to happen.

Dad never hunted again or even shot a gun after that moment. This conversation with dad sank deep in the back of my mind. I understood remotely how generations of traditions and family time spent together were all thrown to the side due to this one look straight into a creatures eyes, as if it was a link right to that deer's soul. So I thought, is killing more important than the hunt?

I am what you would call a trophy hunter. Some will say it is wrong and I am sure that PETA would say that there is a warm spot waiting in hell for me. I don't really care either way. I love the beauty and uniqueness of all the various creatures God has given us. In my trophy room are numerous mounts of birds and various mammals. Some of these creatures are something some people would never get to see if they were not mounted. Because of this, I have gone on numerous hunts just for a specific trophy animal or specific animal missing from my collection. And it tends to be that most of the 'so called' trophy hunts make for way better stories. If you can go out and kill your animal and be done and go home really fast with no challenge, why would you hunt? There is something intriguing about the man who day in and day out goes after game in the shittiest of conditions. It's as if the failure makes the reward at the end so much better if it's a difficult game to obtain.

A turkey for instance, I love to turkey hunt. They give me a rush like nothing else in the world. Anyone can put feed out and shoot a deer off of the feeder or in route to the feeder, but there is something about calling animals and birds that just makes me plain giddy.

I will tell you about a hunt in particular

for turkey. I had not as of yet shot a turkey and my buddies knew a spot and both were great turkey callers. So we made plans to go. It was a nice spring morning and being this would have been my first turkey we brought a video camera to film my first tom going down.

We get there early in the morning, having to walk about a mile back into where we were setting up. We are all tired from staying up late the night before to teach a hunter safety and education class. Now my two buddies on this trip are truly hunting professionals. I am serious, both these guys make their living around hunting in one way or the other. So I know I am in good hands on this hunt. So we truck back into where we are going to set up and they begin to start calling.

They call for several minutes and the toms begin to start gobbling back. It's a cool crisp bright sunny spring morning. We set up against the wall of this old half fallen down small barn. We are sitting on the ground, I have crossed my one leg under the other for comfort and the wait continues.

They call again 'gobble, gobble' is heard from every direction. A couple of minutes go by and out pops a couple of hens. My buddies tell me to sit super still that turkeys can see a penny from a mile away.   I continue to sit. My heart is racing and a few more hens start showing up. They are about fifteen yards away from where we are set up. They are going on about their business. You can hear gobbles from the toms from all over both near and far, but the gobbles are getting closer. I am so excited I can hear my heart pounding in my chest and now a small jake has shown up in the picture. I want to shoot, but my buddy tells me to hold off a couple more minutes that a big tom will show up. And sure as shit, he is right.

Here comes this huge tom, his beard is dragging the ground; it is probably thirteen inches long. He is in full strut, the very first tom turkey I have ever seen performing this mating ritual. I am sitting as still as I possibly can. My heart is pounding and I can hear it and see it through my turkey hunting vest. My foot is now falling asleep from sitting still on it for so long.

The turkey is about fifty yards out, too far for a shotgun to shoot. So I wait, I am not sure how much of this my heart can handle. I feel like I am about to explode from the adrenaline rush. My buddy says, "Get your gun ready." I slowly shoulder my shotgun. The turkeys have no clue that we are right there. The tom is strutting around and trying to pick a fight with the much younger jake. All in just a split second they all become spooked and my buddy elbows me and says, "shoot, shoot, shoot." I squeeze the trigger and BOOM!!! The tom jumps back and is looking like he is about to fall down. It is apparent that I have wounded him.

My buddy gets up and runs towards the turkey and he turns back to look at me and at this exact moment, the moment among my friends I will never, and I mean never live down.

You remember me saying how the three of us taught a hunter education and safety class the night before. Well, the last thing I can honestly say I saw was looking straight into my buddies eyes as he starts laughing out loud looking back at me shaking his head.

I shot the turkey and got up to run after to take a second shot, but my leg had fallen asleep from sitting on it so long. When I got up to shoot again to finish the tom off all you could hear was "SNAP". It was so loud you could hear it on the videotape when we played it back later. So now I am laying flat on my face, my shotgun has come loose from my hands during the fall and has landed about twenty feet in front of me crossing my friend in its flight. I am moaning so loud that if you listened to just the audio of the tape we recorded of the hunt that you would have thought it was some under budget, black market porno. I am franticly low crawling to get to my gun and I can't. I am in tears dragging myself through, what I realized later after I got my clothes changed, was cow shit.

My buddy is laughing so hard at me he cannot shoot the turkey either and the damn turkey flops itself across the river and got away.

So I am laying there, tears in my eyes and my buddy is looking at me like I have lost my ever loving mind, all while he continues to laugh at me. I still cannot feel my foot but I have this God awful pain that is going up my leg and my foot is swelling so bad that my boot is cutting of my circulation.

So here I lay in a pain that I do not know how to explain. The whole front of my body is covered in cow shit from crawling after this turkey, my shotgun is covered in mud and my buddy still has not stopped laughing at me. He tells me to get up, thinking I have just sprained my ankle. And as any nice friend would do he makes me carry all my gear back and walk all the way back to my truck.

I am so sore that I cannot handle the pain. It is actually making me dizzy. I manage to get back to the truck and drive back to town, which is about ten miles from where we were hunting. My pride has kicked in and is taking over and I cannot admit to my buddies the amount of pain that I am in. So I take my buddies back to their house and head back to mine, another fifteen miles. I get so dizzy along the way from all the pain that I have to pull over several times.

I finally get to my house and my foot has swollen so much that it has my boot fully stretched out. I get a ride to the emergency room and the x-ray shows that I broke the top of my foot in four different spots. I am now getting a cast on and all the other extra crap that doctors feel they need to do just so they can charge more. I get all this done and call my buddies that I went hunting with to tell them that I actually broke my foot. They are still laughing so hard that they can hardly talk on the phone.

Later that night I go to another friends house for our weekly poker game. When I wobble in my two hunting buddies are showing off the video and laughing so hard and rewinding to the part where it happens over and over and over. I eventually go watch the video of myself. Now there is nothing to compare to watching a video of yourself moaning like a porn star, low crawling through cow shit, throwing a loaded shotgun towards one of your best friends and watching the damn bird still get away.

I never have and probably never will live that hunt down. I was in a cast for nine weeks and was not allowed to go back to work during that time. My chief of police wanted no part of me wobbling around in a cast chasing bad guys. And after all this embarrassment was about done, I had to finish the second part of the hunter education class the following week. I bet the kids were really thinking. "Those that can, do, and those that can't, teach."

I have been on hundreds of hundreds of hunts since then. Chasing either a bird or animal that I don't have mounted in my trophy room. It seems that the harder I try for a specific creature the more screwed up the stories get. But I think it makes the 'hunt' much more enjoyable and memorable. You can never take for granted that you will kill anything on a hunt or that you will ever find your way out of a hunt.

After thousands of hunts, hundreds of birds and animals, miles of hikes, and hours of hours of training I have had broken bones, been lost, been stuck in mud, vehicles stranded and all while more times than not left empty handed. So I try harder, take it to further extremes and go the extra mile past where most hunters stop and hunt the conditions that most people won't. All to hopefully get that creature or even just a picture of that creature that others only hear about. And as the years have passed by I have learned that I have done way more hunting than killing.

Lost

Most cool stories start out, "I wouldn't do that shit if I were you." And for the most part they are right. I have been told time and time again to never go hunting alone. You would think that after receiving broken bones, frost bite, experiencing hypothermia, poison oak, chiggers and countless other obstacles while hunting that I have faced that I would have learned that by now.

Getting lost is something I never could imagine happening to me. I remember a story of two guys who took a canoe from a bridge by my house down the Red River and just planned on going to the bridge on the southern end of the fork of the river and in less than two miles and after several days they never showed up at their planned finishing point. Emergency personnel had to find them, and when they did they were so disoriented and lost they were les then 100 yards from a road. They were sunburned badly, dehydrated and they were less than 50 yards from a freshwater stream.

I never could imagine that. I mean the sun rises in the east and sets in the west and this is flat land Oklahoma where you can see for miles and miles and miles. But it did happen and I could only imagine thinking, how could anyone in their right mind get lost so easily?

Well the next story explains how either I am not in my right mind or just how easy it is for this to happen to anyone.

It is December in Oklahoma. I have to go to the Northern part of the state on a trip for work. It just happens that where I am going to be at there are pheasants to hunt. I am pretty stoked about this. I have not been able to do a lot of pheasant hunting so I decide I will bring my gear along with me on this particular trip. Now there is snow in the forecast but it doesn't snow much around here in Oklahoma. I cannot remember any time in the twenty plus years I have lived here where it has snowed to any amount at all.

I get my hunting gear gathered up and loaded into my company car, a small Ford Fusion. I put it all in the trunk and try to conceal it behind all my work related tools. The company that I worked for had a strict company policy that stated no firearms allowed in the company vehicles. So for a while my conscience ate at me. I mean I am going on an all expense paid trip to pheasant country and the weather is perfect for it and I am not allowed to bring a gun. So I pondered this thought long and hard and it dawned on me that I am an American. And that America is a nation built on people who broke the rules, so it would be very 'un' American for me to not break the rules to better enjoy my trip. Right? So being the very patriotic

American that I am I figured I had better do what was most American and I snuck along my gun and hunting gear.

I am heading to Guymon, Oklahoma for a very fast inspection for work. My job was to inspect grain elevators and do a safety survey for an insurance company. This was a small account and was not going to take me very long at all to do my job. And when I completed this inspection, my day was complete. All I had left to do was be at my corporate office the following morning. So I left early so that I had some extra time. The drive is from the very Southwestern corner of the state to the very Northwestern corner of the state. It's starting to snow on the trip and there are a couple of inches on the ground. It is a very windy day and the snow is starting to drift on the side of the road and it is continuing to come down. The ground is solid white and it's looking like what could turn out to be one hell of a pheasant hunt.

I finally get to the grain elevator and rush through my inspection. Then I am back on the road to go hunting. I am very excited and I am not wasting any time to get there. It is still snowing and the wind is blowing harder and harder. I finally end up at the public hunting area that I had planned on hunting. This place was located in the panhandle of Oklahoma just West of the town of Hartesy. There is about four inches of snow on the ground and it is looking like this should be a near perfect hunt based on the conditions.

    I get my vehicle parked and dig out my gear and get everything in place for the hunt. I brought a radio to use as a blocker, beings I didn't have a dog with me. I turned the radio on as loud as it would go and I sat it on the end of the area that I planned on hunting. I then walked around to the other side of the public hunting land and was going to use the radio to hold the pheasants between myself and the radio. The noise from the radio would keep the birds down and prevent them from going past the radio, or so I hoped anyway.

The snow is still falling and the wind is blowing so hard that I cannot see anything more than ten feet in front of me. I am starting to feel disoriented but I have just started the hunt so I let my pride take over and try to make the best of the hunt. I mean after all I broke several rules to do this, I had better make it work. About twenty minutes into the hunt a rooster flies up and I take a shot and knock the bird down. I go to look for the bird and it takes me a quite awhile to find it with the weather as bad is it was. When I finally get the bird I start to go back to where I was when I took the shot but I cannot tell where I came from. My footprints are gone! The snow falling and the wind blowing has made it look as if it were a fresh snowfall with no prints at all. So here I stand in the middle of some field and the snow is falling down with hard Northern winds and it is all but white out conditions. I have no clue where I am at and cannot see any form of landmarks either. I cannot hear the radio and nothing is looking familiar. I am cold and shivering really bad. I am getting hungry due to the fact that I skipped my lunch so that I could get to the hunting area faster.

The snow continues to fall and it is well over ankle deep now and the wind is blowing so hard that you could not see at all in front of you. I grab my cell phone to call and it has no signal. I am really starting to get nervous at this point. I am getting the shakes really bad and I am not sure if it is nerves or if hypothermia is starting to kick in.

I continue to try to gain ground but I feel like I am just getting further and further out in the middle of nowhere. So here I decide to figure out a plan. The old acronym STOP: Sit down, Think, Observe, Plan. So that's what I decide to do. After all I am a seasoned hunter, trained in survival, and wilderness camping. How big of a deal can this actually be?

I find a log that has been blown down and is lying down behind a row of trees that will provide me with some protection from the wind. I go to that log and I sit down to make a plan and get my wits back. I looked at my watch and it had been over four hours already. All I could think about is how was I going to explain this to work. I am out in a blizzard, I have no food, no water the only thing I have are the clothes I am wearing, my shotgun, some shells and a cell phone that has no signal. I am really hungry, I have the shakes, and I cannot feel my toes or fingers. I start trying to make a plan to get out of this mess that I have created. I look around and everything looks the same as it did in mid afternoon and I can't tell where the sun is to get a sense of direction. I grab some snow and start to eat it to keep my body hydrated. I grab some branches and build a small wall to block the wind and I sit for a while. I think maybe the

snow and wind will calm down and I can find
my way out.

I sit for over an hour and nothing
changes. But now my body is freezing cold and
my extremities are numb and hurting extremely
bad from not moving and I am getting scared. I
decide to just start walking a straight line and
hope that it will lead me somewhere to get help.
I walk and my body starts to warm up but I am
flat starving and I am hurting allover and getting
cramps really bad. I can barely think rational
and I am becoming paranoid. I end up by some
pecan trees and I look around on the ground for
some pecans, but it is taking more work to crack
them and find them than I can notice benefits of
eating them. So I put a few in my pocket and
decide to continue walking. It is starting to get
dark and I had no light, no way to start a fire, no
food and along the way I got tired from carrying
the pheasant and I threw it down on the ground.

At this time full blown panic has set in. I
could remember the entire place was
surrounded by a fence. It had been six and a
half hours and I was flat lost. Never before had I
felt so helpless, and I didn't know what to do. I
had to be at work in the morning and if they
knew what I was doing I am sure that there
would be future problems. My legs are sore and
I can hardly keep walking so I dig out a spot in
the snow and make a small wall out of packed
snow and I sit back down. I try to think what I

need to do to make it out of here. I know if I
attempt to sleep I will freeze to death. I know
that I can't keep walking aimlessly and hoping.
I take my shotgun and fire both barrels in the air
with hopes that someone would hear it and
come find me. I sit for a while and no response.

I am getting so scared that my eyes are
tearing up and I am starting to have those life
regret thoughts and thinking about all the
wrongs I have still not made right in life. I just
feel like it's over, helpless cannot even begin to
explain how I feel.   I just cannot believe that I
could be so stupid to put myself in to such a
position. After all I teach hunter education and
survival, was in the ARMY, a police officer with
all my training, and I am the idiot unprepared in
the wilderness. I am sitting there lost and scared
and cannot phone for help. So I decide to grab
two more shells and I fire them up in the air......
nothing.

It's now dark and I don't know what else
to do, I have all but given up. I sit back down
and take my gloves off and put my hands
against my chest in my jacket to warm them up.
And when they start to warm back up I stick my
hands in my pocket and when I did I felt the key
remote to my car, so I figured what the hell,
maybe just maybe it would go off and give me
some kind of idea where I was. When I hit the
remote the horn to my car did go off. Now I
know that it will not work if I am not within fifty

yards of my car so I know that warmth is close by, all I have to do is suck it up and find my car.

I get a new sense of energy and willpower. I have confidence like I have never had before. I continued to hit the button and I finally see a glimpse of the lights flashing through a snowdrift. I raced to the car and dug my way through the snow until I could get a door open and get the car started.

I got my car started and turned on the heater and let it warm up. I started to take off my clothes and boots and let them dry out and to get direct heat on my body. I will never forget the cramping and pain as my body began to warm back up. I put my clothes on the vents in the car and they begin to dry off a little. I finally begin to get my mindset back and started to feel a little bit better. Just the hope of making it to a warm meal and nice bed made life all better. I had some candy in the car so I ate that and I took a nap in the car with it running. When I awoke approximately forty-five minutes later I put my clothes back on and dug my car out of the partially melted snow. I then got back on the road and headed to Enid where I had a motel room waiting for me. I left the radio out in the field and didn't even care.

I got on the road and the snow was still blowing down. I had to drive six hours at twenty miles an hour. The whole time thanking God I was still alive. I never again would go out in the woods and not let someone know where I was and not have some basic survival equipment on me.

I learned a very important fact that day. If you have learned something in life and are trained to do certain things, but do not prepare yourself as you were trained and follow your training, is does you absolutely no good.   I was right by my vehicle and could have easily not made it out of the woods. If the worst had happened they would have found my body once the snow had melted, laying so close to my car no one would have understood what happened. Thank God that it wasn't that serious, but lack of planning could have easily made it that way.

It's funny to look back on strange stories like this. This is one of my scariest moments in the woods and I was closer to my vehicle and safety than most other hunting trips. I had all but given up on everything. It just goes to show everyone needs to be humbled and have a wakeup call every now and then.

Old Bird Dog

There are few things in this world that one can appreciate like their old bird dog. They are a tool you use to obtain greater success in the field, your helper when you cannot find your birds, and your companion when you are out in the woods alone. They can be your pride and joy when they retrieve a bird, or flush a covey or hold on that perfect point in front of your hunting buddies. They are your partner and friend, almost like a brother or child. Bird dogs change people and they make you enjoy more than just hunting. Watching your dog on that perfect point or swimming across a pond to bring back a duck is an amazingly proud moment.

When a person takes on the responsibility to own a bird dog they start that unbelievable bond. People start to like a specific breed of dog they have and will never hunt with anything but that particular breed. A sense of arrogance even takes them over how a certain breed is above all the rest. A good bird dog will turn a hunter's mindset to that like a fisherman. The hunt with the dog is always bigger and better than that with out one.

Owning a bird dog is not always fun either. There is no more stubborn of a creature than a bird dog. And there are surely more enjoyable things to do than spend the evening pulling porcupine quills out of them, or having to put them in your vehicle after they thought chasing a skunk around the field when they were supposed to be hunting would be more fun. And as they grow old there is no sadder moment. I know several hunters that when their dog got old and passed away that they quit hunting all together.

My experiences with bird dogs started at a young age. I was thirteen or fourteen when I got my first one. It was an English Pointer. He couldn't retrieve, he was gun shy and he chewed on everything. He seemed to chew on most things that weren't mine and that my parents told me to pick up. And if he wasn't chewing on other people's things he was crapping everywhere. I mean this is why I want a bird dog, isn't it? It didn't take a whole lot of this and I had decided that there had to be something, anything better than this. So after I had had enough, and to my parents overwhelming joy, I got rid of my dog, I never even took him hunting.

I was a young teenager and playing guitar was way cooler than having a bird dog. After all how many women can a guy really pick up when he is out cleaning up dog poop anyway? But a guitar on the other hand, it was almost like a zipper switch. The ladies love you.

Look at some of the most famous guitar players. Had it not been for the fact they played guitar they would be homeless bums with no job and no ladies. But the way they make the six strings twang has allowed them to have women at their beckon call. So as a young hormonal teenager full of testosterone, playing guitar is where I needed to be.

A couple of years later I become friends with some good old country boys. They hunted, reloaded shotgun shells, bass fished and quail hunted with bird dogs. I didn't get to go hunting with these guys right away but I did hang out with them. When I did finally go with them they all had different breeds of bird dogs. It was almost a status symbol amongst them.

I started getting into hunting but didn't really have a clue what I was doing. I would walk around for countless hours and not see anything and if I did it was so far away that it was gone before I got close enough to ever shoot at it.

I still enjoyed the walk and seeing nature but everyone I hung out with were always killing birds. Finally I went with them (them as in my old high school buddies and their dogs). Now this changed a few things. First my slow walk in the woods turned into almost a jog and you could hear my buddies screaming and yelling and chasing their dogs. They did however always bag a lot of birds. It seemed like a lot of work and a lot more screaming because of these hardheaded pointers that they had.

After a few hunts I had it stuck in my head that I needed a dog. Having to always try to be different I thought I needed another breed than what all my buddies had. Every one of them had either pointers or shorthairs. Not one of them had a longhaired dog. So it was set in stone that I had to have a longhaired bird dog.

After several months of looking I didn't have much luck. There were no longhaired bird dogs any where around. I did some research and decided that what I was wanting was an English Setter and I was having no luck finding one whatsoever.

This all changed one day while we were out hunting. There were two guys, who looked as if they were in the military, that were hunting by us and they had an English setter. This dog was beautiful to me. I had to have one. As I was watching these guys they loaded up their stuff and were about to leave. And they were leaving this awesome looking dog!!!!!! The dog tried to follow them and they were throwing rocks at him and shooting their shotguns towards him. I remember the dog cowering down and running off.

This really bothered me. I would go out to the dog for several days and he would just growl at me and run away. But dogs being mans best friend are just like men and the key to their heart is right through their stomach. So I would bring him food every day and he finally got close enough that we were able to rope him

So I now have this dog that I have set in my mind is the breed that I want. There is only one problem. This dog is a nut case. You could not get anywhere close to him or he would growl. If you let him lose he would run off. So far all I had gained was becoming the proud owner of an anti-social marathon runner that does not know how to mind.

Over the next several months my old dog (Ben) calmed down quite a bit, but he was never too sure about anything. He was gun shy and very nervous around people but he was starting to take a liking towards me. I started taking him for rides and he enjoyed that, so that's about all we ever did. If I went somewhere Ben was going too. Until we had a pretty tragic event one day from my stupidity.

I am a young kid I don't have much sense. I snap the dogs leash in the bed of my pick up and as I pull up to a stop sign Ben jumps out dangling by his leash and I run him over not seeing him. This resulted is a very large cut on his leg going all the way to the bone.

I did not have any money for a vet. I tried to see if any of the vets would help me but no one would due to the fact I had no way to pay for it. I felt so bad for Ben. He had been so mistreated before I had him. Here I am just trying to help and just hurt him worse. I end up getting a friend who works at the hospital to bring me a stapler that the hospital uses instead of stitches. Between the two of us we get the wound cleaned and stapled up the best we know how. During Ben's healing process we finally bonded. I had to clean the wound everyday and help him stand up and assist him with his balance as he basically learned to walk again.

When Ben finally healed up we were inseparable, if I went somewhere so did he. He never acted gun shy around me and he soon began to love the hunt. I was as proud as a young kid can be. No longer was I the proud owner of an anti social marathon runner. I was now the proud owner of a different breed of 'Hunting' dog.

It didn't take long and word got out that Ben, my English setter, was a good hunter. Hell he was even stolen a few times. There were some sorry ass thieving drug addicts that thought it was the thing to steal all the good bird dogs in the area for a while. We luckily recovered him and before long Ben had become part of the family. Like my new found son. Hell, there are as many pictures of the family that had Ben in them than there were pictures with me in them.

My senior year in high school during a home basketball game I shattered my ankle into seventeen pieces. I was slowed down a quite a bit, but I still loved hunting. I couldn't run through the field chasing dogs like my buddies, but my old dog Ben would just putt along with me. He was always staying close by and waiting for me to catch up. This is where I truly fell in love with English setters.

As time would have it I got a female setter and Ben and her had some pups. I was home on Christmas Exodus from Army basic training when the pups were born. But during the birthing process the mom died. So me and my wife at the time had to raise the puppies from the first day they were born. One of the pups looked just like Ben so he was the one I kept. As he got older I can remember them two always getting me into trouble.

My neighbor lady had a pool and she would come to my house laughing that my dogs were swimming in her pool when I was not at home. She told me that the dogs had figured out my truck and when it left they would jump out of their pen and go swimming. Then when they would hear the truck start back home they would run and jump back in their pens. I never really believed her but I did do a test. I stayed home and had my wife take the truck, and sure enough the dogs were smart enough to know when I was leaving and to be home before I got back. I hope my daughter doesn't try to be that sneaky!!

There was another time when my other neighbors, who are no longer my neighbors thank God, raised chickens that the redneck husband used for fighting. They had tons of them that were always in my yard, and they were mean as hell. My neighbors and I never really saw eye to eye on much of anything and their damn fighting roosters seemed to make it worse. They would gripe that my dogs barked all the damn time. But they couldn't understand that the dogs were barking at their chickens that were in MY yard. One day I get this frantic call and I am being yelled at over the phone to get my ass home. I don't really know what is going on so I head home. When I arrive my dogs were both out and they were inside the neighbor's chicken pens. The neighbor has a gun out and is fixing to shoot both of my dogs. I am coming home from work as a police officer so I still have my uniform and duty weapon on, and as I walk up the neighbor is now pointing her shotgun at me and is yelling at me to get my God damn dogs. I whistle and both Ben and Spot start retrieving all of the chickens that they so proudly had just killed. So I am standing here and my dogs are being good bird dogs and bringing me the pain in the ass fighting cocks and I can't find it in my heart to yell at my dogs for doing what bird dogs do. But I do get the dogs put up and approach the redneck transplant neighbors about what I need to do to make it right about their chickens.

So I am standing there trying to do my best to make this right and the lady keeps yelling at me, which under the circumstances I guess I had it coming, and she starts to tell me that these birds were like her children. And to be me, like I always tend to be, the only thing that I could think to say back, is "well if they were like your children, how come you couldn't keep them in your yard? And why do you put them in a fighting ring until they die? Is this what you do with your children?" But it ended with me busting out the checkbook and paying too much for their birds that my dogs did kill that were used in illegal game fighting.

Not too long after that I got divorced,

changed jobs and did not hunt nearly as much. I
had no children and the dogs were pretty much
my kids. Hell they even had Christmas
stockings. I would play with them and take
them for walks when I could but we did not do
any hunting for a few years. I had to work a lot
of extra hours to pay for the divorce and that
took upt most of the hunting time. But I did
learn why divorces are so expensive... it's
because they are worth it!!!!

It wasn't very long after that when my
oldest dog Ben passed away. I went out to feed
him one morning and he had got his collar stuck
in the fence and hung himself. He was still
warm to the touch. I cut him down and tried to
revive him but it was far too late. I can honestly
say that that hole I had to dig to burry him in
was one of the hardest things I have ever had to
do in my life. Part of me left that day, but I still
have his pup Spot. Spot is getting old himself,
he is blind, deaf, has a hard time walking around
and just is in typical old dog condition. We have
not been able to hunt for several years and I do
what I can to make him comfortable as he ages.
I have over two decades of bonding with these
dogs. Watching them retrieve, point and the
excitement that they have just going to the field.
There is nothing as cool as walking out to the
truck with a shotgun on your arm and seeing the
dog go bat shit crazy wanting to go hunting.

My best friend has several champion

breed German shorthairs and he swears that they are the greatest breed ever. But I am still happy with my decision to have had English setters for all these years. It becomes part of you and your pride leaks over into your bird dogs.

As I am writing this my pup is now going on fourteen years old, and is in poor health. I have never NOT had a bird dog since I was a child. When Spot passes I am not sure I will ever have another one. The bonds, the memories of the hunts, the just being there to pet and take for a walk after a crappy day are times that can never be replaced. Like an old Gibson guitar, a dependable shotgun or a good fly rod, a bird dog is what memories are made of. It's going to be hard when the time comes to flush a covey of quail or hold point on a pheasant with a dog that's not one of my setters. I am not sure that when mine passes that I will ever give another dog that opportunity. I will probably call an end to some great memories with some of my closest companions, my old bird dogs.

Quack Addict

I love the outdoors, always have. Nature is amazing to me. I am the guy that doesn't need a television set to be happy. I would rather be outside somewhere as far away from humans as possible. I have been this way since I was a child and my hobbies have always been closely connected to the outdoors.

As a younger person I was into fishing. My grandmother was an avid fisher woman so I tailed around with her and that is what we did. We fished and camped all over the place. I didn't do much hunting of any sort until I was a teenager and then it was still very little. I did a bit of quail and dove hunting but not much of any other kind.

As I grew older fishing became boring and I stopped for a while. That is when I really began to be a hunter. I was in the stage of life where it was all shooting and killing for me. My idea of a successful hunt was shooting up a ton of shells and or killing a bunch of whatever it was I was hunting for.

All of us had bird dogs where I grew up. So quail hunting was the 'in' thing. As I grew older it seemed that all of my old hunting buddies had all become poachers or had moved off. Some had become interested in deer hunting and I just didn't seem to fit in anymore. I love the taste of venison but the way they hunt them here is not much of a challenge. I am not saying that I don't go deer hunting, but I go for meat. The hunt is not near as enjoyable to me as what is on my dinner plate. Hunting here in Oklahoma has become so commercialized that deer hunting is quite expensive if you are not the landowner. So this is where I broke the chains of hunting.

The career path I chose was in law enforcement. Not sure it was the right one but it was the one I took, so it is what it is. So every day at work I dealt with the negative side of the world. I learned quickly that first and foremost one man cannot change the world and secondly that no class, race or gender of human is immune to being a victim of the crimes that take place in our society.

I loved my career for the excitement but I soon learned that as a police officer excitement actually   way fewer and further between than what I thought when I got into it. The old saying we get paid for what we may have to do, not for what we actually do is extremely accurate.

What I did see is how society as a whole had taken a change for the worse during my generation. So I become somewhat distant with the world and almost a loner during my time off from work. I am not saying that I don't like to

visit or hang out with people. The truth is I am
actually a very social person. But on my days off
I don't want to party or any of that sort of thing.
I wanted to be alone in a different environment,
preferably outdoors.

Another problem I soon realized I had
was that as a police officer weekends off were
probably not going to happen for me. So this
made it extremely hard for me to hang out with
my buddies. During this time I took up fly-
fishing very seriously. Being alone on a creek
hearing nothing but the wonderful noises of
nature filtered out all of the modern day vices I
deal with daily. This hobby filled a massive
void in my life. But when you are living off of a
police officer salary in Southwest Oklahoma you
can not travel to far away places to fly fish and
in the winter time it becomes fairly difficult to
fly fish any of the waters close to home.

This is where I acquired a new passion.
Somewhere in this time I had learned a bit about
taxidermy. I played around mounting a bird or
two, some fish and a couple of small mammals.
To this day I do not have a deer mounted. It
seemed to me that everyone had a deer head and
I promised that I would not hang a deer on my
wall unless it was damn sure a special one. But I
wanted a 'man cave' or trophy room. So what
was I going to have for trophies? I started going
after what animals I could hunt close to home
and birds that I didn't have. Soon I began filling

my man room with various animals from
trapping and all sorts of game birds.

I had learned that mounting birds was
much easier for me than mammals were. Plus
birds were so much prettier to look at when
completed. But it didn't take long and I had
most of the upland birds and several random
mammals filling up my new 'man cave'.
Turning it into a modern day version of Noah's
Ark, well a dead version, with only one of each
species. But again I had acquired most all the
critters that I could have on my budget. I really
was getting disgusted with hunting. No one
wanted you on their land and tags were
outrageous, and if you set gear up it would be
stolen or damaged when you came back the next
day.

Then a buddy asked me to come duck
hunting with him. He said they were a greasy
dark meat. He further told me if you ate them
you would have to lick your butt to get the
flavor out of your mouth. He said I would need
special shotgun shells, stamps, waders and a
whole list of stuff that wasn't in my budget at
the time. But just like most people I splurged
and purchased a small amount of gear to get
started. It still amazes me how people will
spend money to hunt or fish when they cannot
afford to pay their bills, but this time in my life I
had become just as guilty.

Anyhow we meet the next morning. It is as cold of a hunting trip as I had ever been on. We are very far from where we need to be and there is a ton of crap that needs to be carried and its dark. Not to mention that the wind is blowing out of the North and gusting so hard that it almost knocks you down at times. All the while it is chilling your body down to a cold I was not quite sure how I could ever get used too. So in usual manor I carry all my part of the gear down. My buddy has a friend with him and both are wearing thick down jackets with necklaces around their necks made of leg bands with duck calls hanging down in every direction.

They are toting every shape of duck decoy you could imagine. I was second guessing this whole outing, griping about the distance from point A to point B, how heavy it was and how much money I had to spend to shoot a bird that was going to taste so bad I would need to lick my ass in order to eat it. I have never been accused of being a brainiac, but this was getting a new mark on my already questionable sanity.

We finally get to the river and I am so relieved to be set up only to realize that the work had just begun. Now it is time to get these decoys out on the water and to set up a blind of sorts. The decoy setup was pretty awesome. There were floaters, standing, flying, diving and just about every possible duck you could imagine. The blind consisted of enough cover to barely blend us with the surroundings. It was nothing fancy but building it with just a few branches and weeds piled up actually warmed me up and I was no longer cold. I had learned quickly that duck hunting was a lot of work. It is enough work to at least keep you warm while setting things up.

Now the next few minutes have cost me countless hours of sleep and God only knows how much money over the later years in my life. It is shooting hours and about thirty minutes from sunrise. Light is coming up but it is still hard to see much of anything. It is cloudy, raining and visibility is about twenty feet if that. And out of nowhere comes this lightning fast sound of wind zipping by me so fast I don't know what it is. Then all of a sudden I hear a splash and the quacking of a duck on the water. It was so fast I couldn't even react. I later learned that ducks have been clocked at speeds greater than sixty miles an hour. As this is all happening I am thinking to myself, "How in the hell am I supposed to shoot something I cannot even see?" As I am lost in never-never land thinking, my hunting partners are working their duck calls like magic. The sun is coming up slowly and the lighting is getting better and I am observing mass numbers of ducks heading right to our area in response to the duck calling abilities of my partners. There were so many ducks that you could feel the wind they created as they flew over us. It sounded like a tornado had flown directly over our heads. There were ducks covering the sky above so thick that I was afraid to look up for the odds of being pooped on was greater than not. My adrenaline was racing so fast that I forgot about the cold and was in total amazement of how fast the flock of ducks flew over us. I then was questioning my partners why they were not shooting, all while they are crouching down signaling for me to shut my mouth. And as this is taking place the ducks circle back and come right for our decoy spread.

I can remember like it was yesterday how graceful they just appeared to stop in mid air and began to land in our decoys. I am sitting there looking at the black cloud of ducks and I hear "take em!" By the time I realize what is happening my partners are both shooting. There is mass panic taking place in the flock and mallard ducks are flying in every direction. It was like I was a real life character in the movie 'The Birds.' I see my buddies knocking down birds left and right and I am just watching. One screams, "shoot it" in almost an angry voice and as I look up there is a mallard drake coming strait at me. He is flying directly at me as if he were on some sort of suicide mission.   I raise my gun to my shoulder to take the shot and the bird is moving so fast by time I got a shot off the duck had to be no less than twenty feet from me, and that is when it happened. That one moment in time froze, for I had become a 'quack addict.'

Birds are still swarming in every direction being shot down by my partners. The black lab is running all over thinking he has died and gone to duck dog heaven and I just go pick up my mallard drake. I am holding this thing like I had just officially been titled 'The Great White Hunter.' Proudly holding up one of Gods most beautiful creatures and not caring how bad it tastes knowing I have a place to hang this beautiful bird on my wall.

We ended that hunt not long after.

Everyone got their limit but me. I was being picked on for looking like a lost puppy during the hunt. It did not matter to me, I was still proud. I didn't care that I only shot one bird. As far as I was concerned I had just shot the prettiest mount I would have in my trophy room to date.

We packed out all the gear and walked back to the trucks and I began to understand just why these guys were so into duck hunting. Yes, it took a lot of gear but you took it all home when you were finished so people could not steal it. That is when it dawned on me that most of this hunting took place on public hunting land. So finally I had something fun to hunt and had access to places to hunt without losing my arm or leg for the hunt.

Anyone who knows me realizes I am pretty much a gadget man. So over the next year I acquired all of the contraptions that I could before the next Teal season began. I had made long and hard plans for a September teal hunt. It had been several months since my mallard hunt so I really had the itch. Once again we were packing in gear on public waters. This time the problem was right opposite. It was hotter than hell instead of being freezing cold. But as the last time the birds flew in mass numbers. I am practiced up from dove hunting for the last couple of weeks but the dove were no comparison for the speed of a green wing teal.

They flew in from every direction and before
official sunrise we had already had our limit and
toted all of our gear back out. I teal hunted
every day that first season and before long I was
hitting most that I shot at. I even learned a
recipe for jerky that I really liked by blending
duck, teal and deer together in a sausage type
jerky. I went every morning and was home with
my limit before I normally would have been up
and out of bed. Waterfowl hunting had soon
consumed most of my fall and winter. If I
wasn't in the water shooting I was rigging up
decoys at home, working on blinds, learning
how to call or painting the boat. It was just what
I had needed. Duck hunting provided me stuff
to do on my days off when everyone else was
working and it didn't just have to be during
duck season. I started keeping up with gear year
round so it was in top notch shape on opening
day.

I learned quickly that most of what I did
was extreme. Duck hunting did not need to be
so involved. But it kept me busy and I figured it
couldn't hurt. I began to really appreciate the
mystical ways of ducks. They have the ability to
travel all over the world going to the same
places year after year and to think I had learned
how to communicate with them. I caught myself
going to ponds with calls just to make ducks
come in. Soon I did not enjoy much other
hunting besides turkey and that was just because

I liked calling the birds in more than actually hunting them.   A creature that is smart enough to navigate around the world with out a map, something most humans do not have enough intelligence to do, and I had learned their language. Soon I was on a mission to get one of every species of duck that flew through Oklahoma. I am pretty proud to say that to the date of this writing there are only a handful of them that I haven't been able to hang up in my trophy room.

I remember one hunt in particular. I probably shouldn't admit this story, just for the pure fact of how stupid it will make me look, but

some things are way too funny to keep to
yourself. It starts out on a cold day in January
on a farm pond north of Frederick, Oklahoma. I
have my new girlfriend with me, so of course I
want to be 'Mr. Wild America' himself. The
weather is pretty nasty and I had brought along
my four wheeler so we did not have to walk too
far. I get some decoys out on the water and get
us set up and bust out the duck calls. Now, I am
trying to be a hot shot so looking back I
guarantee I am over calling. However, a small
group of three pairs of hooded mergansers fly
over and boom, boom, boom!!! Birds are down,
hell my girlfriend even shot a hen and I shot
down a drake. The wind was blowing pretty
hard out of the North and the second the birds
fell the wind stopped. In just a minute of
reading you will realize that is proof that God
has a sense of humor. So I am trying to explain
what the drake looks like to my girlfriend at the
time and somehow I end up convincing myself
that they are extremely rare birds. I wade out to
get them and I get her hen and I can't get to my
drake. The water is way too deep and I won't be
able to wade to it. The wind is not blowing at all
now. The pond looks like a sheet of glass. Well
a sheet of glass with a hooded merganser drake
stuck in the middle of it. I don't have a dog and
cannot get to it so I figure maybe the wind will
pick up before we leave and push it to shallower
water. Then maybe I will be able to retrieve it,

but Nooo... that is not happening. So we finish up the hunt and the drake was just where it landed when I shot it. I get all of the decoys picked up and put up and am determined that I have to get that bird. During this same time frame there were several popular shows on TV that were about outdoor survival. I spent a lot of time watching these shows when I was not outdoors. And I remembered one of the shows that had a whole episode on winter water survival. Now this so called learned knowledge from this television show, male pride and being a hot shot in front of the girlfriend all combined with a so called rare duck was beginning to set up for a dangerous combination.

So I conjure up this genius idea and drive the four-wheeler to the shore that is closest to the duck. I stop and strip down naked placing all of my clothes as close to the motor of the four wheeler as I can to keep them warm and yes, I jump in.

I jump in the water in January stark ass naked to get this duck. Now I have been cold before but this was a new level of cold. My man parts were no longer outies, they had become innies and I was shivering and shaking and began to go into shock. I had not yet reached the bird and my body was shutting down. I could not reach the bottom of the lake and I was motionless. I could not function at all. I really thought I was about to die. All the while this woman across the lake is laughing while I am slowly losing all my motor skills and everything is getting blurry.

I am not sure how I did, but I know I did because I am alive today writing this story, but I made it back to shore. I got the warm clothes on and got warmed up and hell my man hood even came back. One of the hardest things I ever had to do was drive away knowing that duck was left on the water.

Looking back to that hunt makes me wonder how the hell I survived life at all. To be that stupid to think I had to have something so bad and to try to impress someone so much that I would become that careless and lucky to escape.

The funny part of it was the next day I went back to that same pond with several hunters and everyone that was with me shot a drake hooded merganser. So I learned quickly they were not so rare after all. But either way I got one mounted and survived the day. It took a few years but I eventually realized that a woman who laughs at a drowning man is damn sure not one to keep around.

As the years would go by when cold weather arrives everyone has learned that I was not going to be home much. I was in duck waters somewhere. I began to specific species hunt. Searching for the few remaining trophies I had yet to get. I was able to do this during the week on my days off all on mainly public waters. Heck even on most private land the owners were more than willing to let me shoot ducks. I did not need to lease land or have someone with me. Now I strongly encourage to never go into the woods alone and damn sure don't act as foolish as I did. I always try to go with someone but when I couldn't I would let someone know where I was going to be and when to expect me back so if I was late people would come look for me. Doing this allows me to be able to go outdoors as much as I need to get the solitude I long for.

All my friends and family started calling me a quack addict. I began to spend the whole year preparing for this season. I scouted ponds to see the species of ducks on the water hoping to find the ones that I was missing on the wall of my trophy room. My trophy room began to look more and more like a still shot of a bird sanctuary. I would have buddies tell me I was insane that investing that much work for a few birds was crazy. I would take them in the trophy room and show them how every breed of duck in its own unique way was a trophy, prettier than any deer could ever be. I soon took pride in having species of ducks that even veteran duck hunters had never seen in this area. Before long my buddies poking fingers would come with me on hunts.

I have two stories that stand out while introducing hunters to duck hunting. The first begins as usual cold weather, long walks, lost of work, and windy weather. My buddy of course rips his waders and they fill up with water and we don't see many birds.

The second, another buddy goes with a group of us to a flooded marsh. We get lost and have to walk a mile section to get to where we should have been. We all just about stroke out during the walk with all of our gear. My buddy is breathing hard and really struggling with the walk. It's a warm day and the mosquitoes are bad. They are swarming in and are so big it is hard not to mistake them for ducks. We don't get many birds that day either. However both of those buddies lived and continue to duck hunt with me to this day.

No other sport do I know of that gives you such solitude but where you can have great companionship on an identical hunt. To work so hard to realize you will probably not kill a lot of birds, to brave the horrid winter elements, to have to carry countless pounds of gear but yet get to keep the final reward is awesome. It is such a beautiful and majestic small creature with navigational skills of a world class pilot that have the beauty of a million dollar oil painting on the wall. It flies with the grace of a ballet dancer and at the same time has the flavor of rotten meat. Another example of God's humor.

Something happens on a duck hunt that transforms most people that go. Working so hard for something so small gives the water fowlers a sense of accomplishment.

I look forward each year to the great migration. Starting with dove and then teal to all the various sorts of waterfowl. Being one with nature even in such miserable conditions becomes a passion to an addiction that in just a season or two can convert most anyone into a quack addict. I have to admit becoming a quack addict has sure helped me deal with the vices and addictions the people on the other side of my career path have chosen. Quack addiction is nothing I foresee going to rehab for in my near or distant future.

Shannon Olson

Sand Bass

My first experience with Sand bass (Morone Chrysops) began about a decade ago. My uncle Joe asked me and my wife at the time to go fishing with him for sand bass. Uncle Joe told me that he had caught this ungodly amount of sand bass the day before and told me it would be well worth the trip. We all decided to go to the Tom Steed Reservoir to catch these sand bass.

I wasn't really all that excited to go at the time. After all sand bass are small fish and I am not really much of a bait fisherman. We still go and it is going to be a short trip anyway. I have to work that afternoon and so does my ex-wife and my uncle. We drive to Tom Steed, which is about an hours drive from my house, and we head up to the dam where my uncle had fished the day before. As we are walking to the water it is rippling and looks like a steady current of moving black water from all the sand bass spawning and jumping in the water. I am not sure how many fish there were but they covered the entire waterway. I began to feel a bit more excited as I observed the mass numbers of fish jumping in the water.

Now as I have already stated I do not like to bait fish and I don't eat fish so I don't really worry if I catch as many fish as the guy fishing

next to me. Second, I am extremely lazy and do
not like having to carry tons of crap long
distances to go fishing and I dang sure do not
like carrying minnow buckets or buckets of
water of any sort for that manner. All that extra
labor to fish almost makes the fishing experience
not nearly as enjoyable. So after the mass work
out of carrying all the crap to the water, putting
on a minnow and staring at a bobber hoping a
fish comes and takes the bait is just boring to me.
When it comes to fishing I seem to have a type of
fishing attention deficit disorder. I need to stay
busy or I lose interest way too fast.

So I get my pole and start to rig up a line
and my uncle stops me in my tracks and tells me
to just put a hook on and a minnow, not to use
any sinkers or bobbers. I think that he is full of
crap, however he is much bigger than me so I
listen, not really. I mean he is bigger than me but
I wasn't really scared of him, it just sounded
good for the story. Anyway I do what he says
and just attach a hook a minnow through the eye
and cast the line into the mass numbers of sand
bass jumping in the water. I then start to rig my
ex wife's line and I have a bite already and I
have yet to even get started on her line. I stop
what I am doing on her line and real in the first
sand bass of the day and then go back to
working on getting her pole rigged up and
thrown out. As I am attempting to do that my
uncle is reeling in his first catch of the day. I

finally get my ex's pole rigged and she casts it out and the second it hits the water the sand bass have already took her bait and she is reeling in her first catch of the day. So in a matter of seconds we have all hooked one each on our very first casts.

This was my first experience with sand bass and with how they spawn. It was unbelievable it was so much fun that it was turning into work. And they continued to bite like that all day long. We lost track of time and it was almost time for us to be at work and not one of us was willing to stop to be responsible and go to work like we should. So we one by one all call into work sick with various ailments that were all made up along the shore of Tom Steed.

After all the various ailments were called in without ever thinking twice we were back to fishing. It is amazing how good fishing can make a bad conscience go away. We fished till it was getting dark and I don't remember the exact number of fish we had caught but it covered the tailgate on my truck several fish deep. My uncle took that mess of fish home for a fish fry and I even got to escape from having to clean all of them too. So as far as I could tell that trip was a total success for me.

This trip was one of the few fishing trips where I enjoyed fishing with bait and never before have I had to make multiple trips back to the truck to carry the fish that we caught. I have not been back to that spot where we massacred the sand bass.

Come to think of it that was the last time I fished with live bait on a rod and real. I did however learn to appreciate how much fun fishing for sand bass while they are spawning could be, no matter what the method of fishing.

Now a few years later a buddy of mine who all but got me addicted to fly fishing calls up and asks if I would want to go sand bass fly fishing. He said he had a perfect spot and that the sand bass were spawning. All I could think about was that trip years ago at Tom Steed. He said that they were hitting on anything white and color and that he had tied some white and pink marabou jig type flies and that they were very successful the day he fished for them. So I got the idea in my mind of the fly he was describing and I tied several up that I hoped were similar enough to what he was explaining so that they would be as successful. The next day I loaded up my gear and headed his way to try fly fishing for the spawning sand bass. Hoping that it would be as enjoyable as the last sand bass fishing trip I had enjoyed.

Now we had received several inches of rain and most of the state was flooded or just recovering from flooding so I was not sure how this would be. But I get to my buddies and we head to Lake Thunderbird. Lake Thunderbird has a nickname of "Dirty Bird" because it is a very muddy and murky lake and with all of the flood water it was extremely murky now.

All the boat ramps were under water and there is not a lot of access to the water and all the shoreline is flooded as well so I am not sure where we are going to get the boat in. As we talk to the locals the waters are so high that they were told not to go out there. So for all intents and purposes we probably were not supposed to be on the water even if we could find access. However, my buddy had this grand master plan on how we could get a boat on the Dirty Bird. His plan worked with much success. I cannot disclose what his plan was but let's leave it alone and just say that it did work. We got on the water and sure enough the sand bass were spawning. The water was pretty calm but you could see large schools of sand bass spawning and jumping in the water. It was so easy we would take the boat to the area and just follow the spawning fish from place to place to place.

As we got to the first group I busted out my fly box and the flies that I had tied for this trip from the advice my buddy gave me were damn near identical to his. And was he ever right about a fly pattern, the sand bass were hitting on them. It was a very unique trip.

Lake Thunderbird is a pretty large body of water. It has over 6070 surface acres and yet we managed to be the only boat on the water.

The shorelines were completely inaccessible so we had this massive body of water all to ourselves. It almost felt like some kind of sin or something to have something so good to yourself even if it's only for a short moment in time.

The water at Thunderbird is dirty but even at that it was beautiful. The lake is surrounded by massive evergreen trees, large beautiful lake homes, and rocky shorelines. To have this to ourselves made it even more beautiful. I had been to the Dirty Bird several times before but never to fish. I have a friend named Travis Linville who has a music studio with a unique name "The Dirty Bird", where I had been on numerous occasions for guitar lessons. At this same studio several local Red Dirt Oklahoma and Texas outlaw bands had recorded and got their start. This made it a more memorable trip for me to finally fish the 'Dirty Bird,' where so much of the tradition from my favorite genre of music had so much influence.

We fished most of the afternoon and did quite well. I got a first hand tour of this massive body of water and it felt as if we were in this far away place. Yes there were houses and in the distance you could hear some cars and the occasional plane fly over but I don't ever recall anytime before in my life going to such a large public lake and not a sole be out there. The only thing out there was us, jumping fish, the occasional bird flying over and piece and quite. To be so close to the city and be able to have such solitude all at the same time is something that doesn't take place often in life.

All the fish we caught we released. We eventually called it a day and we snuck the boat back out of the lake and headed our separate paths. To this writing I have not fished sand bass again but hope to in the near future. Both of the times I have gone were non-stop action. It surprises me that a fish that fun to catch isn't more popular. I have been told that they taste great as well. I have never eaten fish so I couldn't tell but it seems like these fish would be more sought after as a sport fish. Just the two times I have been were so active I was tired when the trip was over. Writing this has made me have the urge to seek after some this year and who knows, maybe I will finally try some and then I can have an opinion of how they taste as well.

It was this very trip that changed me on fishing. I do not fish with any other rod other than my fly rod now. I had pretty much quit fishing for most species of fish other than trout because of the stigma of fly fishing. It seems that trout are what you are supposed to fish for if you use a fly rod. But this trip showed me different. I had just as much fun and action as any other trip with a fly rod and out of a boat. I learned that any species can be caught with a fly rod and that you can fly fish large bodies of water out of a boat with a fly rod as well. I have since fished for almost every species of fish with my fly rod and with a large deal of success. I find it pretty ironic that the Red Dirt outlaw country music that I love so much got a large part of its start at the same place that my unorthodox fly fishing was started as well. I guess all that Red Dirt makes us Okies not so normal in our habits.

It's Called a Trout Stamp Not a Food Stamp

My fascination with fly fishing goes back to my childhood days. I was born in Denver, Colorado as the son of a hard working businessman. As a young child my family moved to Golden, Colorado where we lived until I was about eight years old. My grandmother was the ultimate fisherman, or should I say fisherwoman. There was nothing typical about my grandmother. Grandma smoked like a chimney, cussed like a sailor and had an old stinky sheep dog named Tiki. Grandma drove an old van that was set up for fishing and camping. This van, looking back, was your average hippy wagon. It was maroon in color and had a small kitchenette, sleeping area and dingy golden colored shag carpet. I can tell you from experience that nothing can absorb the odor of an old sheep dog and years of fishing bait fumes like shag carpet. I still remember the long fishing trips going to the mountains with grandma, smelling the old sheep dog and fish bait for hours and hours and watching grandma smoke her cigarette with out ever having to flick an ash. I never really figured out how she was able to keep it attached. She could literally smoke an entire cigarette and all the ashes would stay attached until she finished the thing.

I guess it's kind of a strange thing to remember but this picture in my mind is one of my most vivid memories of grandma.

I am sure there were many trips I do not remember but I do remember this particular trip and I will most likely never forget it. This trip changed me as a person and as a fisherman for life. It all started on a trip to Estes Park, Colorado for some trout fishing and camping. We started the trip in usual fashion, marsh mellows had been soaked in garlic and food coloring, and cans of corn and salmon eggs were ready for bait. For food there were cans of Pork N' Beans, which I was forced to eat cold (I still enjoy a can of cold Pork N' Beans. Every time I taste them it puts me back at the campsite at Estes Park) and some other items for breakfast and drinks.

The trip starts off good. We get to the creek and the typical rants and drills from grandma begin "Shut up, sit down and be still", "keep your damn line in the water, fish can't bite the damn thing if its not in the water", "shut up fish can hear you, you are gonna scare them all away" and my favorite of all "kids are to be seen and not heard". After about twenty minutes of grandma lecturing me she finally hands me a pole, all rigged up, and the fishing begins. I joke about how crotchety grandma was but these times were actually some of the best times of my life. Well back to the story.

  We fished for a few hours and as typical
we conquered the mission to catch a bunch of
fish and headed back to camp.

  During the walk back to camp I observed
something I will never forget. What I observed
has cost me tons of money and time over my life
looking back. There was a man standing in the
river, dressed in strange pants (waders) with a
cool looking vest full of gadgets. This strangely
dressed man was casting a bright green fishing
line really weird over and over and over. When
he finally got the line on the water he didn't
keep it there very long. This man was doing
almost everything that grandma preached to me
not to do while fishing. And my favorite part of
this story is this man was landing fish left and
right. And I'm not talking about little fish either.
I didn't mention this guy was catching fish like
he shouldn't have been to my grandma for the
fear of having the shit slapped out of me. But I

do remember how graceful the guy looked as he was wading in the river out alone one with nature.

We walked back to camp, and grandma got out the can of cold Pork n' Beans. They were served at every meal when we camped. Come to think of it we had a nick name for grandma "granny grunt" because she farted all the time. Years later it dawns on me that it was all them damn Pork N' Beans. Well we got the cooking stuff all set up and then grandma got the trout from our day of fishing and put them in a pan to cook. I don't really remember her cooking them at all. I was a young child still in 'awe' about the guy fishing like he wasn't supposed to and catching all them fish.

I do remember getting lectures about keeping all the food and trash picked up around camp, and to keep it carried to the dumpsters so that bears couldn't get to it. So of course grandma says 'bears' and scares the holy hell out of me, but bears, really? So I cannot resist and I leave some food out to try to lure the so-called 'bears' to camp. The next morning sure enough, bears. There were bear claws all over camp and my breakfast that hasn't been cooked yet was being eating by a small bear cub on the other side of our camp.

Back to the dinner story, I am sitting at camp day dreaming and grandma brings me my plate of dinner. Cold Pork N' Beans, fresh asparagus (we picked in a ditch along the way) and my trout. My trout the very one I caught earlier in the day. My grandma was pretty dang excited and proud as she could be cooking her grandsons very first trout that he just caught on a trip with her. I was pretty excited as well. I was extremely excited up to the point I went to take a bite. As I take my fork and start to get a bite of trout, I look down and my trout is looking up. I mean up, like making eye contact with me. Now what kind of sick joke is this? I am a little kid. I am now crying looking at my grandma and she just busts out laughing at me and she proceeds to tell me that the best flavor of the fish is in the head. So needless to say I ate cold Pork N' Beans the remainder of the trip.

Grandma didn't bring any meat other than the bacon that I fed to the bears on this trip. She planned on eating what we caught for meals. But since that time I can honestly say I have never even tried to eat fish. So at night when meal time came around and grandma ate her fish I sat there as content as I could be eating my cold Pork N' Beans right out of the can.

As I was eating it dawned on me that guy fishing in the river was throwing all of his catches back. I knew me and that strange man had something in common. He didn't like his dinner looking him in the eye either!!! So this trip at age six or seven, I cannot really remember, is where my motto of fishing began.

"It's called a trout stamp not a food stamp".
Now I did not get this motto until way later in
life but this trip is where I set the standard for
my reason for fishing.

I don't recall the ending of the trip but I do
remember that I talked to grandma about they
guy in the water on the way home and grandma
told me that he was a fly fisherman. That didn't
make a whole lot of sense at the time but as in
most everything else I do in life I began to
research the whole idea of fly fishing.

At some point over the next few years my
mom and dad got divorced. I do not really
remember much about this time in my life. I
have this really cool ability to forget things that
are no fun to me. But as years went by my mom
got remarried and my dad found him a new
woman as well. These were some trying times
for a young lad. When we moved from
Colorado with my step-dad, we moved to
Southwest Oklahoma.

I at the time wasn't really sure about my
step-dad and I was pretty positive I didn't like
my dads new woman. I guess that is common
for a young kid growing up in a broken home.

As things turned out it was probably for
the best. I lived in Oklahoma and became super
close and am still best friends with my step-
father. I only use that term so that you know
who I am talking about. I do not believe in the
word step. He was just as much a dad to me as

my real father was. Anyway, I spent my
adolescent years going to school in Oklahoma
and spent my summers and Christmas breaks in
Colorado with my real dad.

　　　Summers were kind of torturous for me. I
had become more and more like my, for lack of a
better word, let's use 'other' dad. This happens
to be a complete one hundred eighty degrees
opposite of my real father. This became a
problem. At a very young age I began to bump
heads with my real father. Dad was a very
successful concrete contractor and that is all he
did, and all he thought about other than the
stock market. So when I could I would take my
paycheck, and I am pretty sure I was very over
paid for a young kid but I wasn't going to
complain about that part. Anyway, I would
walk down to the local K Mart just down the
road from dads and I would get magazines to
read.

　　　It had been a few years since my fishing
trip with grandma but I do remember that I had
found a fly fishing magazine. I also remember
my mind went right back to the trip at Estes
Park with the guy standing in the river. So I pay
for my magazine and run back to dads as happy
as a lark. When I get to the house I go directly to
my room and start reading this magazine about
fly fishing. While reading this magazine I
realized fly fishing was nothing like I had
thought, it was way better. They took all the

pieces of nature and attached them to a hook and made a lure to catch fish.

I had no fly rod, hell I had no clue about any part of fly fishing. But I did observe in the magazine all the feathers and furs that were used to make these flies. So I figured as any normal young kid would that I had better get me a collection of them started for myself. So as I played around with my other afternoon hobby I started to look for stuff to make flies for fishing with.

My other hobby consisted of going out to the creek in my dads yard and hanging out all day. I would pretend I was in the mountains fishing or hunting and I also gold panned with dads old pan. Looking back I always found stuff when I panned. I still have a glass tube that is full of gold leaf, nuggets and garnets that I had found in that creek.

I'm not sure if they were there or if my dad realized that if he sprinkled some nuggets in the creek it would keep me occupied and out of his hair for hours and hours and hours. But nonetheless I found several nuggets and stones. After all this is my story and I can tell it how I want too. So I am going to stick with that fact that I was one hell of a gold panner. I still try to gold pan whenever I get the opportunity. As I grew older I have come to realize that I should have been born a mountain man. Most everything I enjoy involves being alone and out in the woods doing simple stuff like this.

I quickly learned that gold panning and gathering fly tying materials went hand in hand. It didn't take long and I had sandwich bags plum full of feathers. I still have most of them. I began to use some but have since stopped and have kept them for sentimental reasons. Well as things would have it I would ask dad to take me fishing and he would tell me crap like "how many people do you know that got rich fishing?" Which would leave me in disgust and I would go downstairs to my room and read the same magazine over and over and over.

I finally became bored with the same fly fishing magazine and decided that I wanted a new one. So I asked dad if I could go to K Mart and get a new one. Dad answered, "Yes, but don't be blowing money on stupid shit." So I go to K Mart and cannot find a fly fishing magazine but I did find a Rocky Mountain Elk Foundation magazine and for some strange reason I have hung on to this magazine for all these years. I then counted my money and I had what I considered a pocket full of money at the time so I decided to go look at the fishing section. I remember this day like it was yesterday. I can still remember the smell of the different baits and stuff. This was the very first time that I had ever been to the sporting good section of any department store. There was a bargain rack at the end of one of the isles and in the bargain rack was the score of all scores. I finally had found my very first fly tying kit. It was $9.99 and it had a book, the vice and a bunch of materials.

I immediately paid for the magazine and fly tying kit and I was so excited that I ran out of K Mart towards dad's house as if I had stole something. I am as excited as a sixteen year old virgin on his first date. I go barreling into dad's house and he stops me to see what I am so excited about. I show him my kit and he looks at me in disgust and says "I thought I told you not to be blowing money on stupid shit."

What dad had just told me went in one in ear and out the other. I'm sure most everything dad said back in these days kind of went in one ear and out the other. But either way I was so excited nothing he could have said would have mattered to me anyway.

Well things started to get really bad for me at dads this summer. Dad's girlfriend and me didn't get along at all. We never could and never figured out later in life how to see eye to eye. I know I was just a young kid and she was the adult but it was as if she just screwed with me to cause problems between me and dad. This continued for years and years up until he passed away.

Dad's house was a big two-story house that sat in a bunch of trees with a small mountain fed stream in the back yard. The basement was basically a small apartment. I

stayed down there when I was there for the
summers. I had my own bedroom, my own
living room and kitchen. I learned to hide food
in my kitchen and learned how to use the stove
very quick because dad's woman couldn't cook.
We literally ate hamburger helper for every
meal.

I started pretty much staying to my self
in my little basement apartment. I would go to
work with dad and come home and watch
Marty Stouffers "Wild America" which I
recorded earlier in the day when I was at work.
Then I would sit at the little kitchen counter and
would start messing around with my new fly
tying kit.

My first flies were not much to look at
and dang sure weren't anything worth writing
home about. I kept them but they were pretty
ugly and poorly put together. But as time would
go by I slowly got the hang of tying. Before long
I got to where I thought I was pretty damn good.
Looking back I have tied flies for over twenty
five years and I still don't consider myself
anywhere near good, but for that period in time
I thought I was pretty freaking awesome. Well I
finally got the courage to show one off to my
dad. Now dad was not an outdoorsman by any
means. My grandfather was a taxidermist and
dad did hunt when he was younger but in his
adult life if it didn't make money dad had no
interest in it. So I was very nervous about

showing dad my finished product. But I figured what the heck.

Dad was not very good at giving compliments. He was kind of a narcissist and considered himself a bit better than the rest of the human race, so I wasn't really expecting much. But I worked up the courage and showed it to him and he shook his head and said, "You made this? Isn't that about a waste of time? Either way it don't look bad kid". Coming from my dad I considered this a huge compliment.

As years went by I practiced tying and tied thousands of flies. I sold some for extra money as a kid and as the internet became more and more popular I sold some on there and made some extra change to buy hunting gear. I took my tying kit with me most everywhere and I continued to save feathers and fur that I could get my hands on. Over two and a half decades I have gathered pounds of feathers. Do you realize how many feathers are in a pound? Fly tying became my therapy. When I was at dads I tied way more then when I was anywhere else. Something about living at the foothills of the Rocky Mountains and not being able to go out in them made me want to do things to connect with the mountains.

I also learned that it takes a lot of concentration to tie flies. So when dad's old lady was being her typical shit stirring self I could go escape at my fly tying bench and all my worries

went away. So lets skip a couple of decades. I
now have an enormous fly tying set up with
multiple vices, several dozen books on the
subject and damn near every tying material and
type of fur or feather in every possible color
variation you could imagine. So to make this
obsession of fly tying I have even stranger, I still
at this point had never been fly fishing. It is not
till I am in my late twenties that I ever get to go.
I did however continue to tie flies and even took
some formal classes on tying, I still had never
had the chance to go. To this day I have never
even ate fish. I hated to go fishing like normal
people and just sit there all day and I hated
carrying everything to go more than I did just
sitting there. But as fate would have it I finally
go to go on a fly fishing trip.

The first outing was great, we perched
fish for bait to later be used flat head cat fishing.
But I didn't have to carry any boxes or bait.
Everything I needed was right on my vest. And
the constant working of the fly rod saved my
simple little mind from boredom.

I have been on numerous trips all across
America since this time. I have tied thousands
of flies, caught several various species of fish,
some were even in the trophy class all with my
fly rod. It has become such a passion that I
refuse to fish any other way. All my friends
continue to give me hell about all the time,
money and effort I spend fly fishing. They state

to me "You go all the time and don't ever eat any of them, you just throw them back?" The only answer I can ever seem to come up with is "It's called a trout stamp not a food stamp."

Four Wheels, No Brains

Sometimes when I look at some of the things I have done in my life and survived it really makes me realize that God must have a plan for me. I tend to live by the motto 'Go big or go home.' SO… when I started riding four wheelers it was pretty much the same thing.

I enjoyed riding ATV's down the river. I spent countless hours joy riding through the country side either looking for antler sheds in the spring, holes in the river where the big catfish hide out, or just sightseeing. But as time would go by I would soon get the need for speed.

A friend of mine had an old two stroke Suzuki four wheeler that he was getting rid of. Now I had never driven such a thing. I got on this beast and drove it like my other four wheelers that I used to joy ride with and the very first thing to cross my mind was how I was going to kill myself on this thing. I could not believe the difference in power from a four stroke motor to a two stroke motor. They were not even close to each other. The two stroke was in a whole different league.

We begin riding most every weekend on the river racing through sand. Before long I begin to get comfortable racing other bikes and driving through the sand like an idiot. Soon the crazy amount of power wasn't enough for me.

So I worked the quad over. I took off everything
that was not needed on the bike. I shaved off
extra metal parts, stripped the wiring harness,
removed lights, front brakes and shaved all the
plastic. Soon I had a super light super fast quad.
The thing got faster and faster and with all the
extras stripped off. Soon I figured out it could
jump very well. So I would race around doing
small jumps. I really had no clue how to jump or
should I say land. I guess thinking about it I
really never had a problem jumping. I could
always get air time but landing was a whole
different story.

      I remember the very first time I tried to
jump that damn thing. When you're jumping
you are supposed to ease up to the jump then
give it hell at the base of what you are jumping.
I had no clue that was how it worked. So I get
several hundred yards from the hill and go balls
to the wall, driving the thing like I stole it. I hit
the hill and all I can remember is looking at the
bottom of my quad going over me. When I came
to I was laying flat on my back, I had hit the
ground so hard that my wallet flew out of my
pant pocket and landed fifty feet or so in one
direction, my glasses flew off and were about the
same distance in the other direction and the four
wheeler was laying upside down in the river
some hundred feet or so down from where I was
laying.

      I didn't back down. I continued to ride

getting braver and braver and before long I could actually ride. I did a lot of work to that old quad and was super proud of it. The entire motor was polished aluminum, the seat was all redone, the frame was all redone it looked like a brand new piece of work. When I would drive by it just purred and sounding like a weed eater on crack.

So one day several of us get together and ride down on the river and there is this hill we all called the 'widow maker.' It is so steep that some of the other quads could not even make it up. If you were on one of the quads that could make it up you would have to go super fast to make it. Then when you went over the top you would go airborne and get some serious hang time.

Several of us are making the climb and jumps and a couple of us decide that we want a better challenge. There is this clear area on the same hill that doesn't have a trail but there is no debris in the way so we know we can make one. So a few of us truck down to the bottom of the hill and give it hell to get up the thing. It is so steep that our four wheelers want to flip over so we have to lean all the way forward on our handlebars. So far forward that it looks like we are standing up over them.

There are only a couple of us who are able to make it up the new trail and we aren't able to make it up every time we try. There is one spot

in the new trail that is really kicking our butts
and we continue to have trouble at the same spot
over and over. Our tires have begun to leave
ruts in the same spot and they keep getting
deeper and deeper. Resulting in a massive
bump in the trail.

So here is where the fun begins. I get to
the bottom of the hill and I have no idea how big
the rut has grown. I am at the very bottom of the
hill heading to the top as fast as my quad will
take me. I am climbing so fast that I cannot
really tell what is going on. I do notice a crowd
of people standing on top of the hill watching
my dumb ass climb this hill. And in a split
second everything changes. My four wheeler
hits the rut and my tires start grabbing and get
great traction. This gives me extra power and
speeds me up. The front end of the four wheeler
begins to leave the ground sending me upside
down flying in the air the wrong direction going
towards the bottom of the hill. I am beginning to
ask forgiveness for all of my wrong doings as I
foresee meeting my maker in the next few
moments. When all of the sudden I feel this jerk
and then a sudden stop. Now I have no clue
what is happening as I had closed my eyes
scared to death. I open my eyes and begin to fall
from the four wheeler landing on my feet as the
crowd of people begin clapping and laughing at
the chain of events that just took place. As I start
to get myself back together I look up and the

rear axle of my four wheeler is hanging up about twenty feet in the air on the branch of a large oak tree.

I am pretty shook up and all the people watching begin to run down the hill towards me making sure I am ok. There were a few who did think that taking pictures of the four wheeler in the tree was way more important than my safety and well being. The whole time the bike is still running and stuck on the tree. Several of us get together and break it down out of the tree.

That day the bike suffered multiple wounds. I had to replace several parts and get it all put back together. It took me several months but I finally had it all replaced and like new. During this time the same group of guys from the last wreck all decide to go to Little Sahara State Park. So of course I go to try out the repairs on the massive dunes.

When we arrived I was impressed by the riding area. I had never seen that much sand piled up in a riding area. The dunes were way more massive than I had expected and some probably towered a couple hundred feet. I would go with the group riding but didn't hit the dunes the first day. I had some minor issues with my quad that I had to get worked out from all the repairs.

I got my bike back in working order and finally do some riding. We brake for dinner and hang out by the fire for a while and at about two

in the morning we all decide to go for a night
ride. As I said earlier I stripped all the lights and
extras off of my quad. It is a full moon and you
can see almost like it is daylight.

We are all in a convoy going up the
dunes. These dunes have a slope and on one
side it is nearly strait down. I don't realize this
until later but trust me I soon realize and won't
soon forget.

Now I am wearing shorts and flip flops.
The one thing I am not wearing is a helmet. We
are all going up the dunes but the sand from the
bike in front of me is hitting me so hard in the
face that it is hurting. So I back off to create some
distance between me and that quad. There is
about thirty yards distance between me and the
group. The group all stops when they get to the
top of the dunes and just ease down the steep
side. But out off all the friends I have riding not
one of them explained this shit to me! So I am
giving it all I've got and all of the sudden I look
down and there is nothing under me. I just went
mid air over the dune.

I look down and the whole group of
riders are every bit of two hundred feet below
me. Now I have never actually pissed myself,
but trust me if there ever was a time for that to
take place it was now.

    My four wheeler is extremely loud and has a performance pipe that increased the volume tenfold at least. All the while I am flying through the sky the other riders explain to me when I land how they could hear me screaming over the pipe. I have no clue how long I was in the air but if I was guessing it had to be days. I am sure it was only a few seconds but it was damn sure the longest few seconds of my life. I eventually land and it's a near perfect landing. Everyone on the ground had thought I had just jumped that thing on purpose. I was in no way even able to pretend that I had. I was shaking so bad and about to piss my pants. I literally had to pee the second I hit the ground. I didn't think I was going to get my shorts unbuttoned fast enough. I then just stood there shaking so bad that I could not even pull the clutch in to start the quad back up.

The next morning we are all riding again and I am so scared that I cannot ride. One of the guys in the group had wrecked and got a ride out on a helicopter. As a matter of fact the last three times I went riding someone got hauled off in a helicopter.

I didn't ride much after that. Probably over two years went by before I ever did and as fate would have it I didn't get the thing around the block and I threw the rod in the motor. I take that as a sign from God that my days of racing four wheelers are over. I have since bought a big four wheel drive quad that is too heavy to jump and I can just putt around on it like an old man. I figure that if I start acting like an old man I might just live to be one.

You're Not From Around Here, Are Ya?

It's July Seventh, two thousand and
seven. 7-7-07. A buddy of mine is getting
hitched in Southeastern Oklahoma. Another
friend is meeting me there and tells me to bring
my fly rod. He tells me after the wedding is
finished we will do some trout fishing. I'm
laughing to myself thinking he is screwing with
me. I mean, really? Trout Fishing? I love trout
fishing, being from Colorado after all, it's in my
blood. But I'm having a hard time blending
trout fishing and Eastern Oklahoma hillbillies.
But I think what the hell and load up my fly
fishing gear.

This trip was the beginning of many and
there will be many more to come in the future. It
starts out with the five hour drive from the very
Southwest corner of Oklahoma to the very
Southeast corner of Oklahoma. To prepare
myself for the trip, and I suppose for shits and
giggles as well, I decide to watch the old Burt
Reynolds movie "Deliverance" before I go. Now
I know this sounds pretty shallow for me to
stereo type everyone from Eastern Oklahoma as
hillbillies, but nonetheless that's what is going
through my mind.

So I head that way and when I pass
interstate thirty five the scenery changes
drastically. The flat lands of cotton fields have
turned to luscious green rolling meadows and

hills. I make it almost to the little town of
Valiant and I need fuel. So I stop at a town, and
for the life of me I cannot remember the name of
it but there were no gas stations that could take a
credit card. So I am thinking, my first time over
here people are telling me how back woods the
people are and they cannot even take a credit
card. Now everyone I have told about this trip
has warned me of the hillbillies and all the
marijuana crops. I say warn me, I guess the
proper term would be, give me hell and screw
with me.

But before I continue with this story let
me give a brief background of my self. At this
point in time I have been a police officer for
about a decade. And the rumors of marijuana
fields, well they're not rumors. It's true. There
are massive crops of marijuana all over the
Eastern part of the state.

So back to the gas station. It's getting
dark and there are no pumps with a credit card
option. So I am forced out of my truck to go
inside this little rock building to pay for my fuel.
As I walk into the store there are three read
headed men that appear to be brothers and all
wearing bib overalls. I cannot help but stare at
them as the three all stare back at me. The
smallest of the three looks at me and says, "You
ain't from around here, are ya?" I just nod and
go back to my truck to pump my gas. The three
guys then come outside and they go to the truck

that is parked next to me at the gas pumps. All that is going through my mind is these three guys that are toting machetes around like it's the norm must somehow be involved in the cash crop of marijuana, and these big knives are used to cut the plants down.

As I am looking at the guys I am having very vivid memories of a class I once took called marijuana spotting. They showed us pictures of huge crops in Eastern Oklahoma that they would spray weed killer on or they would cut down and burn. Now I can't picture that most everyone would volunteer to help with the harvest of a marijuana field. Hell Taco Bell would probably extend their hours at just the thought of it. But I cannot help but wonder if I need to get my gun from the truck? Should I just get in my truck and leave? What the hell do I do to keep from approaching these guys? I have it in my mind at this point that these guys are in fact real life marijuana harvesters.

As I am about to finish pumping my fuel the youngest or should I say the one that appeared to be the youngest approached me. Now I am standing there like I don't belong, probably about to wet my pants with a dumb founded look on my face and I start laughing. I have this weird thing that happens when I get scared, almost every time I face fear I start to think of things that make me laugh. And this time I am thinking this guy could step right into

a role in the movie 'Deliverance' that I just
watched.

I finally get up the nerve to just see what
happens, and to not look like too big of a wuss.
So I say "howdy" you know trying to blend in
and sound like I belong. Now all of a sudden
the roles have changed. This man in bib overalls
and a huge knife on his hip, that I cannot keep
my eyes off of, comes to me and asks "You down
in this area for some trout fishing?" So I tell him
my story of the wedding and how we plan on
wetting a line after the wedding.

This guy was the most well spoken,
polite, intelligent person you could ever
imagine. He went on about the different spots to
fish, types of flies to use and where the best
eating spots were. Come to find out through our
conversation there is a huge paper pulp factory
close by. He and his brothers were surveying for
the paper company and the machetes were used
to keep the paths cleaned as they went through
them. Either way I felt pretty damn stupid and
more like a judgmental prick. Well we parted
our ways and he said maybe he'd see me on the
creek. As I left I thought to myself, you never
know what a persons story is till you meet them
yourself. So I tried to change my perspective on
what I had preprogrammed in my mind of
Eastern Oklahomans.

I ended up going to the wedding and as
soon as it's over we are racing to the creek. Now

let me tell you this is not what I was used to, or pictured as Oklahoma. As a young child from the foot hills of Colorado this place brought me home. It was beautiful. We went to Beavers Bend Lake, resort or whatever it's called and the mountains are covered in pine forests. Well groomed tree farms used to make pulp for paper I'm guessing. The temperature has dropped at least twenty degrees and the air smells so fresh. There are very few people around and if any there were any they were older fly fisherman on there way to or from the creek with fly rods. After a brief tour through the place we stop at the local fly shop to get our trout stamps. The owners were very pleasant people and full of information of the area and very willing to share their knowledge. We get our set up ready and our stamps and we head out to the lower mountain fork fishing area.

   The lower mountain fork is an amazing project. They have made several areas for trout fishing. Some are catch and release only, some are trophy areas and others are keep what you catch up to six. They have done an amazing job with the rebuilding of these creeks. There are fish that are surviving year round and reproducing. They have made the habitat as natural as possible by changing the water flow to keep the temperature cool and enforce very strict catch and release practices.

We start off at some smaller streams and
practice up on our rusty casting abilities. We
start to catch the fish pretty consistently and we
are able to do some spot and cast fishing. The
water is crystal clear and you are able to see the
fish without much problem when wearing
polarized glasses. The area is all catch and
release so we finally felt as if we were worthy of
moving up the stream to the area where you can
keep some fish. I don't eat fish but my buddy
was wanting some dinner. That would have to
be cooked at a later date because he wasn't about
to talk me into eating any.

This whole "You're not from around here,
are ya?" thought is damn sure going through my
mind now more than it ever was. It's very
apparent that I am not from here. I am dressed
in shorts and a t- shirt, a fly vest and some cheap

water shoes. My shorts and shirt are both dirty from fishing and everyone else along the creek is looking like they are the poster kid for the cover of a fly fishing catalog. I damn sure feel like I don't belong now. It's funny how roles can reverse in the blink of an eye.

This place is like most any place fly fisherman would hang out. There were all the usual stigmas that go with it. There are your older men partnered up with what probably was their life long buddy looking as if they were auditioning to be in the cast of the next Grumpy old men movie. There were also the guys showing up in their over priced SUV's equipped with every possible gadget there is in their fly fishing catalog. Then there were the guys like me who have some gadgets but nothing close to the catalog pinned on our vests. But all the fisherman meshed together. It's as pleasant of a place to fish that there could possibly be. I love this place. I go to various places all over the country and Beavers Bend is hands down my favorite spot.

I remember my second trip. Me and my usual fly fishing buddy are fishing and doing pretty good. We are having as much fun as one can possibly have with our clothes on. We are both on a budget so we're eating vienna sausages, granola bars and what ever else we could bring on the trip from home. We brought fly tying kits with us as well. We planned on

seeing what the trout were hitting on and tying a
bunch ourselves to save some cash. We had
fished all day long and were running short on
flies. So I am at the trunk of the car with a fly
tying vice attached to my cooler tying an olive
wooly bugger. That is what the trout have been
hitting on and it is my favorite and most
consistent fly in my arsenal. I am tying it on the
cooler and the wind is blowing, not real hard but
hard enough to make tying complicated. As I
am tying the fly, two guys pull up in their new
Hummer 3. They get out with all their brand
new name brand gear still all in the package.
They are rigging up and you can hear them
talking about me. I am in shorts and a dirty t -
shirt form a long day of fishing and I don't have
any fancy gear. I am standing at my make shift
fly tying bench so I can get this thing tied up and
get back on the water. Apparently my dress
code was not up to their standards. They walk
by talking to each other about me as if I was not
even there, "How some people just don't belong
on fly fishing waters." I just laugh to myself and
look at the pile of trash they threw on the
ground from all their new gear. As I'm looking
for more trash left on the ground so I can get it
put in the trash can located right next to their
vehicle, I notice that they have out of state tags
and I think to myself "there not from around
here". As if in my few days I've spent here all of
a sudden makes me a native already.

I get my ugly windblown olive bead headed wooly bugger and tie it on my rod and head down the creek from the parking area. I hit the first pool and am not having any luck so I head up stream to a large pool under some rapids. I passed the two fisherman along the way that do not know what a trash can is and I get the expected nose in the air. So I continue to my spot and begin to fish a bit. It's getting late in the day and we are both worn out and are about to call it a day. I cast out and my fly makes this God awful splash and I let it sit for a few seconds and then start a retrieve. As I start the retrieve I get the line snagged on a rock or a log under water. It's my last fly and if I lose it it's time to go home.

I am getting this overwhelming feeling of disgust and right as I start to pout the tip of my rod goes ape shit. The disgust immediately turns to excitement. I have something on the other end of the line. I'm not really sure what but I know I cannot find out nearly soon enough. This push and pull goes on for a while. My fly line is all used up and I'm going into my fly line backing. I don't make it far into the backing and the fish starts to wear down.   As I'm getting the fly line drawn in the fish jumps out of the water and it's a beautiful rainbow trout. I'm so nervous I can hardly hold my rod and the fish is getting worn down but still has some fight left in him. After about twenty minutes or so I have landed this beautiful fish and it's on the shore.

The fish is about a twenty inch rainbow. I was so proud that I didn't release the fish. I took it home to have it mounted. I now have a moral dilemma on my hands. I have this ugly fly I made on the cooler in the trunk of my car that I can keep fishing with and take a chance to lose it or I can call it a day and bring my fish and my fly home and mount them together. I chose the latter of the two. I put my fish in my creel but the fish does not fit. It is so big that about six inches longer than my creel. So I cram it in and the tail is hanging out of the creel. I head back to the car so that I can put the fish in the cooler so it stays in good shape to be mounted. As I am walking back I pass the two 'special' fishermen

and I cannot hold back the urge to go up and ask
them, "Any luck?" Knowing that they had not
had a bite because I could see them from where I
was fishing. They both stood there looking at
my fish and they said that they hadn't had a bite
yet. Little things like this make my day, I love
karma. Well I say that, I love karma when I am
on the good end of the stick.

This same trip we are flat wore out from
fishing all day. It is time to go to the motel and
tie up some more flies for the last day of the trip
and to try to get some much needed rest. This
trip turned out to be kind of like work. Well,
really fun work, but laboring like work
nonetheless. We go to the fly shop and the
owner tells us of a place to fish in the dark for
walleye. Now my mind is thinking,
"Deliverance," just when I finally start to feel
comfortable here. But to strangers from
somewhere else and you are going to take them
fishing in the dark. Hmmm, makes me think
about snipe hunting. Anyway like always, I give
into the peer pressure, well there really wasn't
any pressure, and I just wanted to see what the
hell was fixing to happen. So as fate would have
it I said what the hell and we followed the guy's
instructions and went.

Now I am not going to say where or give
great details of this place. It is a local secret and
I gave the man my word I wouldn't tell. But we
get to this certain spot at dark and cast to the

area that he told us about. This area supposedly
was full of shad at dark and the walleye would
come feed on them. He told us that if you cast a
clouser minnow fly pattern in that area the
walleye would bite them more times than not. It
was crazy out there that night and the creek was
calm with a slight breeze. Not much of one but
just enough to keep the mosquitoes from biting
you all night. The moonlight was bright, bright
enough that you didn't need to use a flashlight.
We tied our clouser minnows on and began to
catch twenty inch walleye for several hours. It
was a blast. There were deer fifty yards away
down the creek looking at us as if we belonged
there, and in my mind I started to feel like I did
belong there. We fished so long it almost turned
into work. I remember the next morning we
both overslept from all the fishing we had done
that day and then night.

    Since that trip I have gone faithfully. At
least twice a year but usually four times a year.
It has turned out to be my get away and solitude
trip. Whenever I am down and out or stressing,
a few days in the Eastern Oklahoma Mountains
makes it all better. Hell I had to stay a couple
weeks at the VA hospital in Denver as my dad
had to undergo brain surgery. Knowing my dad
was never going to be the same was something I
was in no way shape or form ready to handle.
As things got worse and reality hit this was my
get away. I always carry my fly fishing gear

with me and I am in Denver, just a hop, skip and
a jump from the legendary streams of the
Rockies. But I drove back home ten hours and
then got right back on the road and drove five
more to go to Beavers Bend. That was all I knew
to do to handle the situation, and it worked
temporarily at least.

It is just funny to me how we learn and as
we grow how we tend to stereotype people that
we are not familiar with. I am the world's worst
and sometimes I am right, but other times I am
so far off that I almost feel guilty. I have started
doing something kind of entertaining on my
travels now. As I go to various places around
the state and the country I now go to Wal-Mart.
Not necessarily to purchase anything, but there

is this conspiracy that does not allow a person to leave Wal-Mart without leaving a hundred dollar bill there for stuff you don't need. But I have learned that if you want to go to learn about the general population of a certain place Wal-Mart is the place to go. And I must admit in Eastern Oklahoma I have seen the family that is one generation away from having no facial features. The husband and wife both wearing dirty cut off Levi shorts and the husband wearing a wife beater complete with chili stains. The four kids that look nothing like the father following him around wearing nothing but diapers, dirty t shirts and smiles full of silver teeth. And of course the wife walking behind them screaming at the kids, oh and did I mention the wife had black eyes (maybe that wasn't a chili stain). I did see this. This is something you cannot make up. But I also observed several other people that were as normal as a person should be, and people that were there for the same reason I was. I have to say that I have learned something doing this kind of thing on trips. If you go to most anyplace you see some of the same kind of crowds of people. We just tend to focus on the ones that we can stereotype. I mean after all in this day in age is anyone from 'around here' anymore?

Sentimental Nature

I'm a very sentimental person. I appreciate the simple things in life way more than all the drama that goes on in the world these days. I have always been that way and I don't see myself changing any time soon. I'm not a hoarder or anything but it is somewhat a pain in the ass complex to my better half. Every time I go somewhere I steal a rock. I built an ornamental pond full of goldfish in my backyard and it is has stolen rocks that border all sides of it. These rocks come from places such as national forest to the court house that I got my divorce in. I have a rock from most every major event in my life. When I'm down and out I can go sit by that pond with a glass of iced tea and just remember the crazy life I have been so lucky to have lived so far. There is one rock that I picked up and hold most every time I'm struggling to make a decision that is important to me.

It was the day after Christmas several years ago when my hero and friend Oklahoma Trooper Nick Green was murdered just down the road from his home. This particular rock was on the ground beneath him when he died.

Nik was the most honest and decent man I ever met in my life. My daughter's middle name is Nicole in remembrance of Nik. So when I have something heavy on my heart relating back to him helps me do what is right. So far I have to say it does me well.

This strange habit of holding on to items that would seem meaningless to anyone else that sees them carries right on over to my fishing gear.

Now when I say fishing gear I'm talking about fly fishing and fly tying gear. I have all but gave up on fishing with anything but my fly rod. I don't like carrying crap so tackle boxes and buckets of bait is something I quit doing years ago.

But fly fishing to me isn't about catching fish, to me it's about being a part of nature. I have several flies that I've tied that are made solely out of fur and feathers of animals and birds I have killed myself. The only part that isn't is the thread and hook. Those flies are way more special to me than any fly you can buy at a store.

It's not just flies that are sentimental to me. Now I will not fish with any fly I don't tie. I may take one that someone gives me and use it as a pattern to make one of my own but I see it as an unforgivable sin to fish with something I didn't make. I rarely fish with flies that are not made of all natural materials either. Not that I care if others do, it is simply just a strange quirk about me.

All the flies I tie have been tied at the bench I had when I was five years old. Well, minus the ones that were tied creek side or in the motel on a fishing trip. But minus them I've had the same bench since I was a child.

My bench didn't start off as my bench. It was my desk in my room as a little ankle biter. My dad's desk was this massive roll top and as kid I wanted to mimic everything dad did so he got me my own little roll top. It was the perfect little desk to be converted to my fly bench. I have made no changes to it. Just put my vice and stand on it and have purchased some drawers for materials beside it. I have spent thousands of hours at the little desk and every time I open the drawers and see the crayon writings on the inside it makes me smile.

To me being able to hang on to such a

piece of history is amazing. Not just the desk but some of the materials I have are from the 40's. They were passed down to me and I later started collecting rare and vintage fly materials. Every once and a while I will tie a pattern with some without all the modern tools just to see if times were different would I have survived or would I have been the hungry Indian.

My vice is no longer the original AA Sunrise vice I had forever. I literally wore the vice out. I did keep it and hung it up by my bench as a novelty. I mean how many people actually wear out a fly tying vice?

Some of my other tools were either handed down or things I made out of necessity. I do have a lot of modern stuff but if it's something that can be done with the old, I will use them first. After all, why would someone hand you down something if they didn't want you to use it? I mean I still carry Nik's pistol as my duty weapon.

The stuff for tying is in my 'I love me room.' This room is my little piece of heaven. Inside it sits my fly tying roll top bench and across the room is my dad's roll top desk. The walls of the room are covered with what seems to be almost one of every species of North American animal there is a season for. There are some fish from all across America and then my guitars and amps. Next to the fly tying bench sits my reloading bench so if I need a break I can always find something to do in my room. The room has no windows so there would be more wall space to hang animals. It is insulated in sound proof insulation so when the door is closed I am actually in complete solitude. Alone the walls are part of history that I either took part of or things handed down from relatives. I can always get in the mood to tie flies or write down there with very little effort.

This room was designed to be my get away when I couldn't get away. If I had a lot on my mind and want to relax I can go down there, sit at my fly tying bench and just looking around takes everything off my mind. The pride of looking at all the animals, birds, and fish from successful trips just puts a smile in my soul. The bronze star my father received or the novelty can of 'Fish Assholes' my grandma gave me just makes it that much more rewarding to me.

When I'm able to get away and hit the waters or the woods I seem to have a problem. I take care of things so I have things forever and I still use everything I have. My buddy Kenny Baker, for example, makes the most beautiful hand carved turkey call you will ever lay eyes on. They look like something that should be under glass somewhere to just look at but that's the only turkey call I will use anymore. If I'm going to get a turkey I would much rather know I did it using one of Kenny's call.

Of all the things I'm sentimental about

my fly vest is the worst. Now I don't really care
for the 'vest wearing and greater than thou' fly
fisherman. And I like how they have made
lanyards that hold everything you need so you
don't have to look like a snooty old fly
fisherman that has so long been stereotyped. But
I cannot seem to let go of my vest.

I wore the same vest for years and kept if
for over two decades and finally decided I
wanted a new vest. So I gave my old vest to one
of, if not my best friend when I got him into fly
fishing.

So I started wearing my new vest. I
purchased the vest on a clearance rack in La
Junta, Colorado on the last trip to see my dad
before he got cancer. When dad was in the
hospital I had to quit my job to help take care of
him. So I sat at the hospital for days and when I
started having a hard time dealing with
watching my father slowly die, I would go down
the road to the fly fishing shop and look around.
My tippet holder was purchased one of the
afternoons that dad was having a bad day. I
couldn't deal with it and when he went to sleep I
went down to the fly shop and it took me over
four hours to buy something. I just looked
around and visited with the guy behind the
counter. Me and the guy at the fly shop began to
get to know each other during those weeks and
some of the items I got from him will be carried
around with me forever. There is a pair of

forceps that I purchased on a trip to North Dakota in some department store at age 8. There is also a pair of nippers I purchased that day I caught the biggest rainbow trout I'd ever caught with a fly rod. There is a picture of my grandma who taught me to fish and another of my daughter who I love more than life itself in the pocket closest to my heart. And hung on the back is my wood net that almost crippled me one time when I slipped and fell in the water and it rammed right into my spine.

That's what the outdoors does for me. It takes the most simple things and makes them super special. And all the little secrets and trinkets I've kept for so many years I now realize is just my way of hanging on to the good memories of my life. There's a story to tell by all the stuff that would be all but useless in any other but my hand.

But all the little things either for work or play that I hang on to are those special reminders of why I do what I do.

The solitude of fly fishing has made the grieving in my life sometimes so much easier. Just being out there alone or down stream from your fishing partner. When all you hear is the sound of water flowing makes it so easy to think. I love the feeling of landing a fish and using the old crap on my vest to make it all come together.

My grandma and Dad are both probably looking down on me and saying, "That boy sure wastes a lot of time on the water with that old crap." But maybe just maybe that is my plan after all. You never know just how long it takes for something great to happen out there. Hell, the longer I'm out there the more of a reason I can justify grabbing a rock for my pond.

Hog Wild

If there is one animal I had to pick out as my favorite close to home hunt, it would definitely be feral hogs. I live in a very rural community in Southwest Oklahoma and the Red River is less than two miles from my house. My lifelong friend Jerimy farms several hundred acres of land by the red river and the feral hogs wreak havoc on the wheat crops. So I have had many opportunities to hunt wild piggies with Jerimy.

Now before I go too far in this story I should first give an explanation of my friend Jerimy. Jerimy and me grew up together, went to school together and have remained close

friends through our adult lives. Our fathers
even passed away the same day within an hour
of each other. So to say we are close is an
understatement.

Jerimy is the person who taught me to
hunt, helped me get my first bird dog, hell we
even learned taxidermy together. So over the
last several years of outdoor time with each
other we have learned a lot about each other's
hunting habits.

Now if you ever go hunting with Jerimy
you will soon learn one thing. This boy can flat
shoot. I mean he is the best natural shooter I
have ever met in my life. Now keep in mind
that I am a police officer and have been for
several years. I have served on SWAT teams, in
the army and taught shooting classes and hunter
education classes for years and I have never met
a person who can shoot like him. He is an
amazing natural shooter, I am pretty sure he can
shoot fly shit right out of a pepper jar.

Jerimy has introduced me to hunting as I
know it and pigs are something we hunt for a
lot. Not only is hunting these feral nuisance
animals fun but it is also necessary to protect the
wheat crops. You cannot imagine the amount of
damage these animals can cause to a crop in just
a matter of a few hours.

I have been out where pigs destroyed
several acres of wheat over night. The field
looks as if it was plowed up by a drunk that

couldn't keep a straight row. Just looks like freshly turned dirt with no sign of any vegetation left in it. I have also seen where pigs have rooted around and continued to dig in the fields for moisture and dug holes so deep that tractors were not able to make it across and the field required some excavation work to be done. So all of this said, when your lifelong friend is an avid hunter and a farmer you get to hunt hogs a lot.

I have been on numerous styles of hunts. From hunting with dogs where they track the pigs down and pin them and then you just walk up to them and put them down, to assisting on hunts where government hunters showed up in airplanes and helicopters to take out mass numbers of pigs causing major damage. But hands down my favorite way to hunt pigs is with a bolt action rifle from a long long distance away.

Jerimy and myself have both built long range rifles. The main area we hunt has become extremely familiar, so we have a pretty good idea when it comes to judging distances at this place. So now we go out there and set up and see how long of shots we can take. There is always room for improvement and these pigs reproduce faster than bullets are assembled so it's a never ending supply of live moving targets to increase our shooting performance. We have shot a lot together and with one spotting the other it is not uncommon for shots to be taken out well over seven hundred yards. They have even been taken over a thousand yards out.

Now I am not going to lie to you and tell you that I have always shot pigs at these great distances because Jerimy would call me out on it. But I have improved greatly on my shooting and long range hunting is not at all as complicated is it used to be.

Now when it comes to hunting stories I have realized that it is way more fun to talk about the failures and complications on trips than the successes. I mean after all if it was always easy and went as planned it would not be fun for anyone to partake in. So for this story I am going to take you back to my very first long range rifle hunt with Jerimy. It was not a failure, it was a spectacular hunt, a great shot, but it was a failure to me all at the same time.

Most of my life I have been a shooter. I picked up a .22 rifle when I was a young child and began hunting birds as a teenager. As an adult I became a police officer so I shot pistols and shotguns all the time for work. I loved to shoot pistols and even shot some competition but as far as long range shooting I never had done a lot of it up to this point.

I shot M16s in the Army and shot an AR15, the police version of an M16, as a duty rifle when I was a patrolman but I had never shot anything with high power optics. So Jerimy helps coach me through building my first long range scoped rifle and we decide to go hunting piggies.

The hunt takes place in the middle of a several hundred acre green wheat pasture bordering the Red River to Texas. On the Texas side the landscape is pretty much baron prairies with enough mesquite trees randomly placed that I wouldn't want to walk through them. So if the pigs want to eat any kind of crop they cross the river into Oklahoma and steal our crops like some kind of illegal alien mooching of our system.

We get set up in the later part of the afternoon and pigs begin to cross the trickle of water we call the river and they are onward bound climbing the bank to Oklahoma seeking greener pastures. They get to the Okie side of the bank and climb the steep embankment and make it to the wheat. It was a spectacular sight to say the least. We are posted up on bi-pods several hundred yards away watching the hogs through binoculars and they just keep coming over the top of the riverbank. There has to be at least fifty of them all walking in a single file line evenly spaced keeping perfect time, as if they were trained solders on a military pass and review. I am getting the shakes I am so excited. I have yet to draw blood with my new rifle and I am just waiting on the word from Jerimy to shoot. Finally as they keep coming across and I

see so many I don't know what one to try and
take Jerimy nudges me and says, "Get ready."

   I start to get even more excited. I see at
least fifty targets and I have a new rifle so this
experience should be a great one. Jerimy is
looking at me and laughing because I have the
shakes and I am breathing so hard that it sounds
like I just ran ten miles up hill to get here. And I
am just sitting there getting more and more
excited as each second passes. Jerimy nudges
me and nods to me to tell me to shoot. I nod
back to acknowledge him and I tell him that I
will start on one end and he can start on the
other.
   So I have it in my mind that we are going
to just plow this line of fifty plus pigs down
shooting from one end to the other meeting in
the middle leaving a line of pork a half mile

long.

But this is what actually took place. Jerimy nods, I nod back he takes a shot and the pigs go ape shit crazy running around in every direction. So I am beginning to see that my half mile long pile of pork is probably not going to happen. One pig is running a straight line down the small farmer road through the field and I have him in my sights. I am looking at this monster through my new scope and it is a genuine mammoth of a pig. I am serious this thing as an absolute hog, no pun intended.

Now I am nervous, shaking and can hardly talk from the excitement. I have this ginormous pig in my sights. I decide to take some deep breaths and get myself together and calm down. I get the pig in my sights, the scope is perfectly aligned with the vitals of the pig, I take another deep breath and squeeze the trigger. BAMM, the pig is down with a perfect shot. I am not wanting to wait to see the victim of my rifle and I am ready to see this monster up close, but Jerimy is wanting to hold up for a bit and thinks that more pigs will be coming up soon.

Finally Jerimy gives in so I will shut the hell up and we go look at my pig. As we are approaching the pig Jerimy is laughing at me asking me where my pig is. The only pig there is one about eighty pounds or so. So I know that it is not mine. I am getting pissed thinking that I

missed mine and that Jerimy shot this little pig
and I didn't even get one.

As Jerimy is explaining in between
laughter that this is the only pig shot in this spot
and that it is mine. He takes my rifle and shows
me where my scope was turned up all the way
so my little pig, standing at the edge of the
wheat crop where the wheat was about a quarter
of the size of the actual crop, looks like a
monster through my scope that is zoomed all the
way up.

I am pretty sure that I won't live this hunt
down with Jerimy anytime in the near future.
But it was not the last of my pig hunting, nor the

last of my dumbass stories. I have greatly improved my shooting and spotting ability and I have damn sure learned how to adjust my scope. There for a while I was certain that Oklahoma had a special breed of rabbit that was close to cattle size. I am kind of disappointed to realize that all the animals in my neck of the woods really were not giant size. But nonetheless I have improved as a pig hunter, and even took up trapping them as well. I have trapped hundreds of them with Jerimy and at numerous other places without him.

I enjoy each hunt and trapping as much as I did that very first time. I try to hunt the hogs as much as possible to protect the croplands and to provide some pork in the freezer. I have began to get way more excited when I shoot a seventy or eight pounder than the three hundred pounders, mainly because the smaller ones make a fine meal after they get out of the smoker.

There is a lot of talk about the flavor of wild game, but I promise you if you shoot a pig in the seventy pound range that has been feeding on wheat, you won't find a better thing to put on the smoker and slow cook. The very first time you try it you too will end up being Hog Wild.

The River is Rising

There are some things that take place in nature that will forever change the way you think and act. When you go head to head with nature, the power of Mother Nature is something that can never be taken lightly, as Mother Nature sometimes gets cranky and shows us her wrath.

This particular incident I am talking about was not in any way a tragic event, but had I not been with someone who knew what was taking place it could have turned into a few closed casket funerals. That is if they would have ever been able to find our bodies.

We are on Turkey Creek, a small creek North of the town of Olustee, Oklahoma. The creek has a beautiful area called Red Rocks where the whole bank is large rock boulders towering above the creek with large deep pools of water below. These are areas that have been turned into local swimming holes with some of the large rocks used as diving boards. The creek turns into a normal dirt, brushy grass bank farther downstream and that's where we fish.

The creek is deep enough and holds enough water that some large catfish linger around and with some stink bait you can land them most any day right before dusk. The fishing is no local secret to people, the creek is well used and you can tell. There are trails stomped down through the weeds making it easy to walk to and from. The trails are littered with worm containers, empty beer cans, cigarette wrappers and all sorts of other crap left from inconsiderate asses that show no respect for other people's property. But as with anything else Mother Nature has checks and balances about keeping areas clean.

Just like forest fires every few years keep the forest underbrush clean, massive amount of water can wash all the rubbage and litter downstream never to be seen again.

Me and a buddy of mine Raymond, who has since lost his life to a tragic fishing accident, and some other friends all plan on an all night cat fishing trip to Turkey Creek. We trapped several hundred minnows the days before to make our own special stink bait. We took the minnows, dried them out and then cut down a bunch of cattails out of a nearby pond. We ground them together and made some of the best dip style stink bait I had ever used.

We gather up all of the other stuff we deemed necessary to use on the trip, lanterns, chairs, rods and reels, tackle boxes, bait containers, bug spray, you know all the stuff we tote to a fishing trip. So that if we catch any fish, just to get all of our gear and fish back to the truck will take several trips. We take all of our gear and we start down the old worn paths in search of a nice flat spot large enough to hold our gear and give us a place to sit. When we finally find a spot suitable for our needs we get the lanterns fired up so we can see before the sun goes completely down and it is too dark for us to see.

We spend a couple hours fishing and storytelling. I am certain that most of the world's problems were solved on that creek bank. If only we would have brought something to write them all down with so we could have remembered. We hung around shooting the shit and catching a fish every now and then, but mainly just enjoying the nice spring evening.

It is a beautiful spring evening. It is warm outside but it's by no means hot. There is a slight breeze, just enough to keep the mosquitoes from carrying us away but not enough to mess with our fishing lines and screw up the fishing. To the North is a thunderstorm. It is far enough away that we can hear the thunder but it is not all that loud. The storm is heading away from us so we feel no need to worry about it anyway.

The fish really begin to bite so we quit paying attention to the storm and start concentrating on our fishing lines, catching fish and re-baiting our hooks. It is now getting close to ten thirty or eleven at night and all of the sudden the wind just stops. It didn't just fade away and ease up, it just stopped out of nowhere. The fish quit biting all at once and it

just gave a weird feeling to all of us. We
continued to fish and watch our poles for the
next several minutes and we did not get one
single bite. It was odd, like the fish could tell
something was about to take place.

Then all of a sudden, I hear this loud
roaring rumble up stream. Not a roar like lions
living amongst us but something similar to an
old locomotive grinding the rail right above us.
The sound is getting closer and closer and is
louder with each second. It is very unnerving
especially with the wind stopping and the fish
not biting. The totality of the circumstances has
the hairs on the back of my neck standing strait
up.

I have no idea what is taking place, I
observe Raymond packing all of his gear up
rather franticly. He looks at me with a very
serious face and tells me if I don't want to lose
my gear I better get it all picked up. I still have
no idea what the hell is going on but I know
Raymond isn't serious often so when he is I
probably better listen.

The noise is getting extremely loud. It's a
dull constant roar or rumble. It is so loud you
can feel it. The only thing I can compare it to is
when you are parked at a red light and next to
you is a car with some kid wearing his hat
sideways. He probably needs to pull his pants
up so the crack of his ass won't show, his car is
an old hoopty but has a few grand in rims and

tires and the radio is blasting this constant boom, boom. The boom is so loud that it carries into the next beat vibrating everything in sight and you can feel your heart beating with the rumbling crap he has confused as music. That's the feeling I am getting standing there on the bank. The overwhelming vibration of the ground and even the noise is vibrating the air.

It is total darkness out, other than what light our lanterns are putting out there is no other light. The cloud cover is enough that no stars are shining through. We have shut down all but one of the lanterns to carry our gear out so we have the dull light of just one lantern.

Raymond tells everyone there to get up the bank, he is still somewhat frantic in his voice and is telling us to do this but still has not told us why. But if Raymond is being this persistent we all know that there is a reason and not one of us question the man. Raymond is always joking around so when he is serious we are damn certain there is a reason why. So we all gather up our gear and head to the top of the bank some thirty yards up. We all go around the trail and get on top of the bridge. I look down and I can see a reflection off of my minnow bucket that I had forgot downstream. I start to go back down to get the bucket and Raymond grabs my shirt and tells me to just let it be that there is no way I am going to be able to get it.

I am so confused about what is going on

that I am not sure if Raymond is screwing with all of us and just pretending there are monsters and stuff out there. But the roaring rumble is getting louder and louder and it feels like my heart is now beating in unison with the rumble. And after all Raymond can't make the wind stop blowing and the fish to stop biting. I am not a superstitious person by no means and don't believe in all the things that go bump in the night, but with all that is happening around me I am really starting to question those beliefs. And just at this moment, I am looking like a deer in the headlight to Raymond wanting an explanation of what the hell is going on and Raymond screams, "look boys!!!!"

Raymond wasn't playing at all, what I was about to see was probably one of the coolest things I have ever witnessed in nature. The creek where we were located was as calm as it was we showed up. The waters remained calm. The creek was probably about thirty feet across and it was as still as a sheet of glass. Raymond was getting excited and had went to his truck and got a portable spot light and shined it down the creek about a hundred yards down. With the assistance of Raymond's light, you could see this giant wall of water coming right towards us. The roar of the water became louder and louder and the ground beneath our feet was trembling and shaking. You could literally feel it all the way up the bridge. The wall of water moved closer and closer washing down everything in its path. The wall was every bit of ten feet tall and standing almost vertical racing towards the bridge we were standing on.

We all stay on the bridge looking at this amazing sight, not paying any mind to our safety. Hell we never seen anything like this before so we had no clue if it was about to take out the bridge or not. But we all stay up there looking down at the water. The giant wall then scooped up my minnow bucket. The bucket was tumbling around and was going up the water as if a professional surfer had taken the reins of the bucket and made it bank up the wall of water. Then it just disappeared going down stream with all the litter that was on the banks before it.

The water kept racing and before you know it the whole creek had risen several feet. The water was up in the trees flowing extremely fast and bubbling this dirty brown stuff that made a sheet of brown foam bubbles on top of the water. Resembling nothing even close to what the creek looked like just a few seconds before.

We watched with amazement, learning to appreciate just how much power the water had and discussing how the fish quit biting realizing what was about to take place. All the while six grown adults had no clue what the hell was going on. It never even rained on us. The rise of the water was all from a storm that was at least two counties to the north of us.

The fishing was over for the night so after watching the water show we loaded up all of our gear and headed out. I returned the next day to look at the creek, still not believing what took place the night before. All I could think about was how I just witnessed something that appeared to be out of a biblical story with Moses being the lead character, not me and Raymond.

When I returned the banks were washed clean. The only things on them was a few piles of brush and weeds washed together looking something like a small beaver damn. But there was no trash whatsoever.

That night was damn sure a sight to see. What I would have done to have a video camera along. Without any warning and no rain for close to a hundred miles and this massive water flow to come our way was no other word but amazing. Had Raymond not been there it is hard to tell what would have took place.

I love it when odd things like this happen on outings. You can watch all the television and read all the books you want to about nature but until you witness something like this you cannot even closely imagine the power of nature until you become part of it.

Port Isabel

I've never really put a lot of thought into relocation. I am pretty content living right here in Southwest Oklahoma. After all, where else in the world can you live that if you travel in any direction it immediately looks better than where you came from? However there is one place that always questions my loyalties to this Southwest Okie town, and it is Port Isabel, Texas.

Port Isabel is one of the oldest cities in the extreme Southern part of Texas. Historians have said that Spanish explorer Alonzo De Pineda was recorded visiting the place as early is 1519. It is a small town and the 2000 census showed the population to be at around 4800 people. The town is on the Southern most tip of Texas, the last stop on dry land before crossing the long bridge to South Padre Island. It's the perfect little vacation town without all the nonsense that takes place on the island. When you come into town the main focal point is the beautiful lighthouse that was erected in 1852.

Port Isabel has all the necessities needed and as long as it's not spring break it is very affordable. But even then who the hell would want to be there during that time that is older than twenty one years of age.

I have a very heartfelt love for Port Isabel and South Padre Island. All of my life I have been on trips down there. As my granny grew older and the cold weather of Colorado began to take its toll on her she moved to South Texas. So whenever we kids were out of school our parents would take us to granny's where we could see the island, enjoy catching some true lunkers of fish and be part of a tropical culture we would never see at home.

My first trip to Port Isabel took place when I was just a kid. Me, my sister, mom and dad all pile up in mom's Volkswagen Rabbit car. It is a tiny extremely compact car and it's the brightest and most God awful orange color you can imagine.

No shit, this car is so damn bright and ugly one day we were going to see my dad at work and there was a large bull in the field where he was and when it seen the car it become so totally pissed off that it started snorting and scraping its feet on the ground, like we were some barrel at a rodeo with a clown behind us tormenting him. Actually the thing was about the size of one of them barrels and as many rodeos that I have been to in my life I have never seen a rodeo clown dress that bright and gaudy.

But anyway we piled in to make the fourteen hour journey to the Texas tropics. You never realize how small a vehicle is until you put a young boy in it with his older sister for fourteen hours. After the long trip we finally get to granny's house and when I seen all the water and palm trees the fourteen hour ride with my sister seemed all worth it.

Granny lived in this small little campground that had some motel type homes, a pool area and an activity center. The place was right on the water with a marina less than fifty yards from us.

At this point in my life I had never seen this much water or even seen a ship that wasn't on television. So when you are only nine or ten it doesn't take very much of that to just impress the hell out of ya. So we do all the meet and greet stuff that you do when you see your granny for the first time in several years and then I head to the water just as fast as I can get there.

Me and my dad both go to the marina closest to granny's and we take a pole each that granny let us use. We had a box of fresh shrimp that we picked up at the bait shop across the road from the marina. We bait up and throw out our lines and it doesn't take very long at all and we are catching fish. This was pretty damn awesome as I remember.

The first fish I caught was a little bitty fish, covered in spikes and when I took it out of the water the little thing puffed its body all up like a balloon. It was damn sure something you are not going to see where I had been fishing before. I caught some sort of eel, I don't have any idea what type. As soon as I seen it I cut the line. I don't like snakes and anything that looks like one fall into that same category. There is something about an animal that has no legs and can move faster than me that just scares the willies out of me. We also caught a bunch of saltwater catfish. The locals were telling me that these fish were called crucible catfish. They cleaned one for me and showed me where the bone on the top of the fishes head looks like a cross with Jesus on it.

As most good things come to an end so did this one this trip. I came down with some sort of a flu bug and was sicker than a dog as everyone else was out having fun fishing and playing in the water. It became so bad that my mom had to take me to the doctor. We get to the doctor's office and he decides that I need a shot. Now I wasn't on the same page as he was and thought this trip was bad enough already what the hell did I want a shot for. When the doctor started to give me the shot I tried to run and I hid under the table in his office. The doctor and my mom were pretty pissed off and when the doctor bent down to get me a second time I kicked him right in the face. Wow Jesus wow!! If you ever want to see how mad you can get a parent or how strict your parent really is, do some stupid crap like this and I promise they will show you.

Well that all passed and it was our last day. We went to the island and picked up shells,

surf fished for flounder and then we went to
Mexico to do what became basically a ritual
when we went down there. We stocked up on
vanilla, medicine, chikla gum, gamesa cookies
and all the other crap we didn't really need, but
beings we were there we better have a year's
supply of it all. So we gather up all these so
called needed items and put them into the
already crowded car and start the trip back
home.

　　The trip back home always seems more
crowded, longer and damn sure more
uncomfortable than any trip ever does going to
the destination. But add bags of oranges,
grapefruits, a few pineapples, bags of peppers,
jars of vanilla and whatever else you can pile up
and you can surely make a trip seem like it's an
eternity.

　　We made several trips back over the
years. I never stopped enjoying the seashell
shops, going to Mexico, the fishing and just
everything about the place always was fun for
me. But grandma grew older and we moved her
home with us to Oklahoma where mom could
take care of her until she passed away. We
never went to South Texas during those years.

　　When grandma passed away she didn't
want to be buried so mom decided to take her to
the island and place her where she loved to be. I
couldn't see a better option for a woman who
spent her whole life fishing around America. I

wasn't able to go on that trip with my parents but to me it made Port Isabel and South Padre Island just as sacred. So let's take this a few years forward.

It's January 2010 and I am at home in Oklahoma and the weatherman is predicting ice storms like we have never seen before. Now if you live in Oklahoma you will soon realize that the weathermen here are very dramatic and when they get on a rampage you never know just how bad it will get. But again if you live in Oklahoma you also know that the weather is capable of doing most anything imaginable as well. The weatherman is saying a major system of historical proportions is heading towards us and that we could lose power for days and maybe even weeks.

All the hype of the storm and the thoughts of being without power for days or weeks just doesn't sound like any sort of thing that I want to participate in. So I discuss the idea with my parents of all of us going to Port Isabel. And we all agree to head south for winter and we will just tough it out on the beaches of South Padre during this ice storm.

This trip we take my truck, which has way more room than that ugly ass Volkswagen we took as a kid. It is me, my mom, my dad and my niece and we are south bound. The trip is not like most trips where you are in a hurry to get from point A to point B. Actually we are not in any kind of hurry and just as long as we are South of the storm we are just fine.

   We make it a long day of driving and rotating drivers every now and then so that we can all get a nap in and be rested up. We stop at every cool little spot along the way. One of the places being Hico, Texas, where a guy who was the nephew to a man who he thought we was Billy the Kid gave me a wooden nickel with Billy the Kid on it. I know things like that are for kids but I guess I am just always going to be a kid at heart.

   We finally get to Port Isabel and the palm trees are blowing in the wind. It's late evening so the lighthouse is all lit up.

The air blowing in off the fresh saltwater is just relaxing to your soul. We unload our stuff at the motel and go for a late evening stroll enjoying the warmer tropical air. Actually we were in shorts strolling around and the locals could tell we were tourists as they were all bundled up thinking it was cold as the front had pushed down there as well. But it was a total different climate to us. We were all super warm.

The next morning we head to the island. Mom wants some flowers left out for granny. So I get the flowers and wade out into the Gulf of Mexico as far as I can and toss the bouquet of carnations out as respects to granny, the lady who taught me everything imaginable about fishing.

We walk the beach for a while, picking up

seashells, poking jellyfish with sticks. The wind is blowing so hard that we finally call it quits and head to the truck. The wind blew rampid the entire time we were on the beach. I felt like I had been sandblasted by time I made it back to the truck. I brought my fly rod with me but it was way too windy for me to even think about attempting to fly fish.

The next day I go to the local fly shop and get some saltwater flies. Now I refuse to use store bought flies but I had no saltwater fly fishing gear so I had to give in and purchase some, but as fate would again strike I didn't get one single opportunity to even use one. The wind blew hard as hell the entire trip.

With the wind blowing like it was we decide that we will get off the beach and head to the Mexican markets to find some shit to drag home. We literally drag home a whole load of crap. We had a truck load of oranges, pineapples, vanilla, and Mexican gum. All the same crap we drag home each trip down here. As we are going through the market I see this metal knight and I just have to have him to put in my trophy room with all the animals. I am so certain that I need to give this guy a new home that I buy him at the beginning of the shopping trip and have to carry him around all day. Me and my niece are having fun joking around and cutting up and have begun to get somewhat out of hand. Mom is getting agitated with us and we are all tired so we head back to the truck.

When we get to the truck and mom is resting up, I leave the knight with her to guard and she states how she seen a cross that she wanted for her yard. So after she confuses the hell out of me describing what cross it is she wants me and my niece go back to get it. As we go back in there is a fortune teller at the gate that will not leave us alone. He keeps coming to us and I tell him I am not interested. He continues to persist and comes up to me and says, "How are you today sir?" in very broken English. The only thing that I can say is, "You're the fortune teller, tell me how am I doing." I then realize I am sick of the shop tellers trying to take advantage of my tourist dollars. The fortune teller didn't seem to appreciate my humor so we soon left before I really pissed him off. We get to where the crosses were and picked out the one that closely resembled what mom had described to me. As I am this Mexican man begins talking crap about me to his partner in Spanish. I know I am about as white of a person that you will ever meet, but when it comes to the Spanish language I can converse pretty damn good, so I understood everything he said.

I am pretty damn agitated with this guy and when I get agitated sometimes I do stupid crap. So as we are walking around I see a Virgin Mary statue. I thought it looked cool so I purchased it to put in my room as well. So here are me and my niece walking around this Mexican market place carrying a Virgin Mary statue and a large metal cross. I cannot resist the pressure and have to go back to the place where I got the cross and the merchant who was talking shit in Spanish. As I come back he is still talking about how stupid Americans are so I give into the pressure and stoop to his level. I know it's a Mexican tradition to have the Virgin Mary statue inside of a bathtub as a yard decoration displaying the love for the Virgin Mary. So I do one of the tackiest things I probably have ever done and I approach this guy with my Virgin Mary and ask him if he knows where I can find a blue bathtub. You talk about pissing of the locals. The guy is flaming mad so I decide if I want to live through the day I may need to just get the hell out of dodge.

Now my distasteful comment went all over this guy so I am exiting the place as fast as I can. The last place I want to piss off everyone is a Mexican border town. After I realized what I just said I couldn't believe how distasteful I was but if anyone deserved it, it was damn sure this guy. So I get to the truck alive, laughing at my dumbass but silently asking God to forgive me for my tasteless comments.

I never did get to fish on that trip and I still have this major urge to go back again soon. The place is beautiful and all the local people are great to deal with and treat you like you are at home. The prices are not inflated at all and in the wintertime it is mainly older people enjoying retirement the same way that I hope to someday. I have a large box of flies I have tied for my next trip down there that will hopefully take place this fall. I know one thing if I get to go down there again and make a fishing trip out of it, I won't be going to the local border town and pissing off the locals. I figure you can't get away with that too many times.

Round One

I always laugh when I think about people with their addictions and how they got started. I cannot imagine anyone puffing on their first cigarette and thinking, "man this is great I think I want another one". It is probably more like they are gasping for air, choking, coughing, and turning green all the same time throwing up and their head spinning. What part of that would make you want to try it again? But more times than not most of our addictions were an awful experience the first time we tried it. To me hunting kind of fit into this same category at first. I never really could understand why or how I became so addicted when I look back to the very first time I went.

It was back several years ago when I was barely old enough to drive. I had shot some firearms a bit, had spent a lot of time in the outdoors, camping fishing and the such but by no means would I be what you would call a hunter.

I went to a very small rural farm school. Southside School was a very neat school, only a hundred students from Pre K to twelfth grade. And because of having so few students the school eventually had to close. I was scared to death about leaving this special little school and wondered if I would ever meet any new friends.

We had to transfer to a new school and at this new school is where I met some of my lifelong friends.

The new school was still a very small school, there were only twenty people in my graduating class, but it was bigger than then Southside was. I started hanging out with some of the new friends I had met. We worked on trucks, played basketball and before you know it we were going bird hunting. All had become well at the new school.

It's the first day of September, it is hotter than donut grease outside. My new friends are taking me on my very first dove hunt. Hell it was actually the very first real hunt I had ever been on. It is opening day of dove season, the first fall hunting season in Oklahoma and you would think it was a national holiday by the way everyone was getting all worked up for it.

We all load up in my buddy Tracy's little pick up. Tracy had two trucks but his hunting truck was some small foreign made truck like a Toyota or Nissan. It was a compact truck but we all would pile up in the thing and that truck would go anywhere. I don't recall us ever getting that old truck stuck. And trust me, we would have tried too.

We are all piled in the truck and go to this field that I assume we had permission to hunt, but knowing us back then you can never tell. Along the way I cannot promise that no doves were shot off of high line wires either. Looking back it amazes me how little respect for hunting laws we had. I don't think we really thought of what we did was wrong either. At least we out grew that part. But back to the story, were piled up and end up at this large cotton field that has a tree row of tall cotton wood trees on the southern most border that was planted many years ago as a wind block. We all get out of the pickup and are dressed in camouflage looking like we are going to war. We have several boxes of shotgun shells that the guys had reloaded themselves so I can almost promise that they were a tad bit supercharged with powder. It is extremely hot outside and we only brought some pops with us to drink, so we each get our pops, shotgun, shotgun shells and are about to head our separate directions in the field.

I have never been dove hunting before so I don't really know how I am supposed to set up or what to do other than to shoot at them as they go by. So I get a few pointers from them and they decide where we are all going to set up. Tracy seen a small water hole he wanted to sit at and Jerimy wanted in the tree row and on the other side of the field not too far off was another cotton wood tree that they decided I should set up on. We all begin to part ways and as we do Tracy opens up a can of cherry flavored Skoal tobacco. He gives Jerimy a dip and then asks me if I want one. I had never tried it, but I figured they both seemed to like it so what the hell I would take a dip.

I pinch off a dip and put it in my mouth between my gums and lip like they did. I grab my gear and start to walk off, thinking I am going to enjoy my first dip and my first hunt. Boy was I wrong, I don't make it thirty feet and I am getting dizzy and my mouth feels like it is on fire and I have a bubbling feeling in my gut like I am about to shit myself.

I am walking thru the cotton and I am wanting to get rid of this God awful shit in my mouth but I figure as much as they liked it maybe it would settle and get better in a bit. So I decide to hold it in my lip for a while longer.

As I am walking the first pair of doves of the season, and as far as that goes the first pair of doves for my life fly overhead just in shooting range. I aim at them and shoot, and holy shit I soon realize just how fast doves can fly. I also begin to think doves are cocky birds, when I shot they flew back over to taunt me and let me know just how piss pore my shooting really was. I shoot at them again and they were right, my shooting was piss pore.

My shot was way off the mark but the birds are flying right towards the tree row that Jerimy is hiding in. Jerimy sees them and boom, boom. He shoots both birds, they fall down and just two shots. I am watching this in somewhat shock how easy it was for him to knock down these super fast moving birds.

I head back in the direction I was going to set up on the large cotton wood tree and as I am walking I am getting dizzier. I am getting worse by the minute, my mouth is burning, my head is throbbing, my gut is still bubbling and I feel like I am going to throw up or shit myself. I am not sure which one and wouldn't be surprised if it was going to be both. I am too embarrassed to ask what to do with the dip, I kind of feel like a mangina not being able to handle it while both of my new friends are just as content with their dip as they could be. I have this large amount of spit forming in my mouth that I can hardly talk without it dripping out, but I don't spit any of it out, for some strange reason I don't want to waste any of it. So I just keep suffering and let the nasty crap stay in my mouth.

I get about halfway across the field and I see some more birds flying towards us. I yell to Jerimy and Tracy to let them know about the approaching birds and all I hear is Jerimy screaming. I am trying to take a shit, do either of you have any toilet paper?!!!

I didn't really know what to think, I had never even took a dump in the woods and to think were out hunting and hadn't been there very long at all and he already had to take a dump. I am just laughing to myself. I yelled back to him that I didn't. As I am yelling some of the spit goes down my throat compounding

my problem of dizziness and really made me
want to throw up even more now. And I am
thinking to myself, who the hell carries toilet
paper everywhere they go?

 I still cannot see Jerimy but the birds are
getting closer to his tree row and they soon fly
over the exact spot he is at. Just as the birds are
flying over, out of nowhere pops up Jerimy with
his pants below his knees and his white ass
hanging out one hand on his gun and the other
wiping his ass. He had improvised a piece of
toilet paper and has what appears to be a piece
of his t shirt in his hand wiping his ass at the
exact same time he is shooting the over head
dove with just one arm working the shotgun,
and wouldn't you know it he knocks the dove
out of the sky. I am laughing so damn hard that
I swallow the remaining spit that was in my
mouth.

 I cannot breathe, I am gagging, starting to
get a really sick feeling in my gut and I cannot
walk. I am trying to make it to the tree I was
heading to but every step I take makes the world
underneath me just start spinning and spinning
and before you know it I am falling to me knees
puking my guts up. I begin to get the shakes
and am covered with goose bumps and begin to
get the chills. It's over a hundred degrees
outside and I am all of a sudden feeling cold. I
fall flat on my face and black out. The last image
in my mind is Jerimy shooting and hitting flying

over doves while wiping his ass with part of his t-shirt.

I am not real sure what took place next but I blacked out completely and fell down in the middle of the cotton field between two rows of cotton. I was dressed completely in camouflage clothing, so how they found me I have no idea.

I don't know how long I laid in the cotton field or who found me. Knowing these guys how serious about hunting they were, I am sure they both got their limit before looking for me. But nonetheless they do end up finding me. I cannot say I remember any part of me getting up I just remember being back at the truck drinking water and throwing up for what seemed like hours.

I am still white as a ghost, throwing up, dizzy and my buddies are laughing so hard at me for not knowing how to dip that they have tears in their eyes. It seem like it took forever for the sick feeling in my gut and the awful headache to go away.

I finally stop puking long enough that we can head home for the day. I don't really know what was worse, the pain in my head and gut from the dip or the vivid picture of Jerimy wiping his ass but still able to hit the birds flying overhead. I mean hell, I couldn't even hit them with one hundred percent concentration.

There was a lot of crap talking that took

place on the way home that afternoon. I will forever remember the horrible sick feeling in my gut from the Skoal. To this day chewing tobacco products make me want to vomit when I get the slightest whiff of their odor.

I got home and went to bed trying to recover from the gut ache I had given myself and call it a day, hoping that tomorrow would be a new day and I would still have my new friends. Hoping and praying my dumb ass didn't scare them off on the first outing together.

I get up the next morning head to school and it was a new day. The first thing the guys said was they were going hunting after school and asked me to come. Not a word about me getting sick was mentioned. I jumped for the opportunity to go with them again. Not knowing if they really wanted to hang out or if my dumb ass was just comic relief for them. Either way I went and on that next day I shot my very first dove and still to this day, not a season has passed where the three of us have not been on a hunting trip together.

I am not sure how or why I ever wanted to hunt again, especially with these guys or why they would even want me back out with them. But since that day, the three of us have been lifelong friends more like brothers. We all still share the same passion for the outdoors. I probably owe both of them some gratitude for the Skoal incident as well. After all they have probably saved me thousands upon thousands of dollars by the horrible experience with tobacco making damn sure I would never want to try it again.

25983925R10100